BACKSIDE OF NOWHERE

BACKSIDE OF NOWHERE

A Novel by

Sharon Sebastian

ISBN 1-58500-540-1

1stbooks – rev. 5/17/00

About the Book

Backside of Nowhere: A mystery about hope, romance, murder and a juke joint just across the county line called the Delta Blues. Outcast and abandoned, a family in a nowhere Texas town finds courage to overcome poverty and humiliation only to face a very real threat to their lives as the past comes back to haunt them. Life is rarely as it seems in a town on the outskirts of nowhere and when events begin to smolder under a hot, Texas sun...somebody is sure to get burned.

CONTENTS

The mid-1950's were both a simple and a confusing time. But then, it could be, those were just circumstances peculiar to a small town -- buried deep in the middle of nowhere -- called Cedar Grove. They had a saying there -- "If you think you've got it bad, there's always somebody down the road a bit who's got it badder." Small town opinion…salted with dubious grammar… always seemed to hold particular sway. Especially, when people got to nattering on about other folk's misfortunes. And, to hear some of them talk, there was one small family that lived on the edge of town -- that put "bad" in a whole new category.

As the story goes, hardship was drawn to their door step like metal to a magnet. But, the fact of the matter was, they never had much to begin with…and from the looks of it…they never would.

1)   UNCOMMON BEGINNINGS

In the dead of night, riding the back of an ill wind -- trouble once again blew itself into town. Unhinged and on a rampage, it swirled fiercely and menacingly about in the midst of heavy and darkened thunder clouds as a violent storm whipped through the small Texas town of Cedar Grove. Old street lights dimmed as the small town hall quaked in the storm's fury. The clock on the top of the building read 2:35 a.m.

On the opposite side of town, a relentless rain pelted heavily against the window of a small, dilapidated house. A sudden gust of wind raked a tree limb across a window pane as a huge crack of lightning lighted up the blackened sky. A small gasp could be heard as a tiny figure bolted up in bed and stared fearfully through the tattered curtains that hung in the window. As another bolt of lightening seared across the heavens, the tiny figure quickly ducked under an old patch-work quilt for safety.

Inside the small bedroom, the frightened child huddled under the old quilt as the storm raged, sending streaks of light across her small bed. Suddenly, a loud shattering crash caused her to sit up. This time, it was not the thunder. It was the sound of glass crashing against the exterior of her bedroom wall. Frantically, as she wiped her tears, the young girl listened intently to the sounds of her parents' anger.

On the other side of her bedroom door, in the living room, the sounds took on a more ominous form. A heavily intoxicated man, in a fury, glared at his very pregnant wife. His senses debilitated by his drunken stupor, the man held tightly to an empty whiskey bottle as his body weaved, unsteadily, back and forth.

Enraged and out of control, he exploded once again in anger as he slammed his hand hard against a lamp, sending it reeling. He turned the bottle upside down for another drink of cheap courage, only to find he had drained it dry. Deprived of yet another drink, the empty bottle served as further evidence of his dire plight. He was both out of luck and out of rot gut whiskey. His face, twisted and contorted into a mosaic of anger, Joe Castle hurled the empty whiskey bottle through the air, smashing it hard against the wall as the small house once again shuddered from the raging storm.

"How the HELL do I know it's even mine, Camille!?" he demanded of his terrified wife.

Shivering and in tears, Camille Castle stood there looking at her husband. With her worn cotton dress stretched tightly across her swollen belly, it was obvious that she was due at any moment. It was not a good time for her world to be in turmoil. Alone and vulnerable, she summoned as much strength as she possibly could. She then spoke to her ranting husband in a controlled and decisive voice.

"I understand your pain, not being able to find a job, Joe. I do. It's a hurtful thing. But, you will not shame me by denying your own family." For once, Camille had decided to stand her ground.

"I know you married me," she continued, "because I was pregnant with Cassandra, even though you refused to believe she was your child. Well, she is your child and so is this one," she insisted, struggling to keep her voice from rising in anger. "But, don't you worry," she said with unwavering conviction, "I'm not going to use this baby to make you stay. You've been wanting a way out. Well, now I'm giving it to you."

In his alcoholic haze, Joe Castle looked down at the floor. Her cool frankness seemed to have a stabilizing affect on him. His voice turned more desperate than defiant as his words came out haltingly. "I...I never wanted it to come to this, Camille. The truth is...you're better off without me." Remorsefully, he looked at her, "I just wanted to win one game, just enough to set us straight. But, it all went to crap. I gotta get outta here," he said as his words revealed more than his drunken despair.

"A wife...kids, ain't nothin' but a rock around my neck. I got no family anymore."

Camille looked at him, confused, "What are you talkin' about, Joe?"

"Don't you hear what I'm sayin'? I lost everything!" he yelled at her, his thoughts seemingly disconnected. "It happened so fast. Things got outta hand, turned real bad on me. I tried, I did. It just ain't in the cards, Camille. There's nothin' left. We're out here livin' on the backside of nowhere."

Clearly reaching the end of his rope -- he looked at her, threw his hands upward into the air for added emphasis, and then with a bitter finality, declared -- "I give up. You hear me? I...give...up!!"

Peering through the bedroom door at this disturbing scene, was little six-year-old Casey. She had seen her parents fight before, but there was something different about it this time, something frightening. A chill ran through her small body as she saw the futility in her father's face. When he picked up his coat to leave, she bolted through the door into the living room to stop him.

"No, Daddy...no," she yelled, "don't go!"

He was stunned at first to see her. He then bellowed, "Casey, get back in your room. This ain't none of your business."

"Is too," she insisted, tears streaming down her small face, "is too some of my business. You're my daddy...you can't go."

His mind and emotions blurred with the cheap alcohol, he had no words to respond to his young daughter. With nothing left to say, he picked up his coat and fumbled through its pockets as he headed for the door. Unable to find his car keys, his anger once more intensified. Exasperated, he rifled through each coat pocket, angrily ripping one open, leaving it dangling by its threads.

"Where are my keys!?" he bellowed.

Camille glared at him, "That car is mine. You're not gettin' it."

He looked at her -- ready to meet her head-on. Then, just as quickly -- as if he had suddenly been drained of all his energy, he shrugged his shoulders.

"What the hell. Keep it," he said, acquiescing. "It's nothin' but a piece of junk. It's falling apart like everything else around here."

Having summed up the whole of their existence in one short sentence, Joe Castle stumbled out of the door and out of their lives. As the door closed behind him, Camille and Casey stared at it, dazed.

The sound of the cylinder clicking in the lock suddenly separated them, irretrievably, from the world in which they had existed only moments before. Trembling, Casey turned to her mother.

Camille looked at her small daughter. Seeing her child's innocent face, she felt the deep hurt of failure. Her chin began to quiver uncontrollably. Her body began to shake. As she fought back the tears, her eyes shifted downward to the wooden floor. Large shards of the demolished whiskey bottle lay in pieces across its warping floor boards. Smaller splinters of glass from the bulb of the busted lamp lay sprinkled about like crystallized snow.

Her mind and body in a state of shock, she felt as empty and shattered as the broken whiskey bottle. Without thinking, Camille kneeled down and began to clean up the broken glass around her.

As she reached to pick up a sliver, its thin, jagged edge sliced into the palm of her hand. Startled, she dropped the glass, drawing her hand quickly back. It was too late. The injury had been done. Her warm, red blood dripped to the floor below as if her very life were seeping out of her. Numbed, she looked at her bleeding hand. Tears overwhelmed her as her pain turned to sobs of desperation.

Casey felt a wave of anguish sweep through her little body at the sight of her mother's deep hurt. Her own emotions somewhat tempered, she slowly walked over to her mother and wrapped her small arms around her -- doing her best to comfort her.

Her mom looked up and smiled weakly. She caressed her daughter's innocent face.

"Don't worry, Angel. We're...we're gonna be all right."

Suddenly, Camille grimaced in pain and clutched her swollen stomach.

Frightened, Casey called out, "Mommie!?"

"Oh...oh my God. Uh, Casey, honey? We've got to get in the car, okay?

"Go get your raincoat. Hurry, honey."

As Casey started towards the closet to get her raincoat, her mother braced herself against an old chair, digging her fingers into its worn fabric. Gripping the back of the chair, she doubled over in agony and yelled out in pain as a large clap of thunder rattled the house. Camille struggled towards the door. She called out to Casey.

"Sweetheart, forget your raincoat. We've gotta go...now!"

Terrified, Casey rushed to her mother's side.

***

Like most small towns, many of the roads around Cedar Grove were little more than oversized dirt paths...and once some poor soul was on them...rain and darkness tended to sorely complicate matters.

That night was no different. As the lightning flashed, the pulsating red lights of an ambulance and sheriff's car could be seen glowing eerily through the pouring rain. Anybody driving by that night could see that some unfortunate family in an old car had smashed into a tree.

With the rain saturating the darkness, a new born baby's cries were barely audible as the thunder rumbled over head. Standing a distance away in the shadows of the whirling red lights, wrapped in a blanket, was Casey. She watched helplessly as her mother and the baby were being loaded, bundled together in one blanket, into the back of the ambulance. She could hear her mother's voice as she called to her over the pounding rain and rolling thunder.

"Casey! Casey!" she called out frantically for her young daughter.

Seeing Camille's distress, a sheriff's deputy moved as fast as he could through the thickening mud, over to the ambulance, to reassure her. With each step, his feet appeared to sink farther and farther down until it oozed up around his pant leg. Slogging his way through the quagmire, he was finally able to reach her.

"Don't worry, ma'am," he told an anxious Camille. "She's a little shaken up, but she's fine. I'll bring her to the hospital myself."

Camille clutched the deputy's hand, "I thought I could make it. But, the pains were coming so quickly. I...I lost control when the baby started to come..."

In an attempt to move things along, the ambulance driver nodded to the deputy that he had everything under control. He then looked at Camille.

"You just hang on now," he consoled her, "we'll be takin' you and the baby the rest of the way."

As the driver closed the rear doors to the ambulance, Camille disappeared inside. With everything secured, the driver

then climbed into the front seat of the ambulance and took off --
sirens blaring.

Frightened and feeling very much alone, Casey stood there,
watching in the pouring rain -- uncertain if her life would ever
be the same after that terrible night. It had all become way too
complicated for a little six year old girl to understand.

***

A few short days later, at Cedar Grove Hospital, several
nurses bustled around in the hospital's nursery. Their very
movements seemed to create an oddly organized and systematic
flurry of activity. Exemplifying the epitome of efficiency in
their bleached white uniforms and heavily padded, white shoes,
they made very little noise as they moved from one crib to
another. One of the nurses came to a stop next to one of the
cribs. She leaned down over it, gently lifted up a small bundle
and held it securely in her arms as if she were handling precious
cargo.

Several feet away from all of the other babies, off to the
right of the nursery's large, plate glass window and positioned
next to a wall -- a very tiny, but beautiful little baby girl slept
peacefully in one of the hospital nursery incubators.

Though separate and apart from the others, the tiny baby
was far from going unnoticed. Standing on a chair, peering
through the nursery's window, with her face pressed hard
against the glass, was Casey. She strained upward as high as she
could, tottering on her tiptoes to get a better look at the tiny
figure in the incubator. For all of her effort, she could only
manage to get a clear view of the top of its tiny head. Shifting
her body slightly, she once more pressed her face hard against
the glass, cocking her head to the side. When one of the nurses
saw her small, contorted form smushed up against the glass, she
smiled with amusement and quickly repositioned the incubator
for easier viewing. Relieved, Casey eased down off her tip-toes.
She quickly wiped the moist smudge of her face print off the
glass with the palm of her hand.

Fixated on the incubator, she stared through the glass at the baby, finally getting her first good look at the tiny newborn. Casey was not quite sure what to think.

She suddenly felt her mother's gentle touch on her shoulder.

"Your baby sister is a fighter, just like you are, honey." Casey looked at her mother and nodded in agreement -- even though she did not fully grasp what her mother was saying to her.

"She got quite a bump on her head," her mother continued to explain, "but the doctor says she's doin' great. She's just got to stay in the incubator a while longer."

Casey stared curiously at the strange little creature in the plastic and metal cage. It was so different from what she expected. She looked at the other babies and then back at the tiny, little bundle. Her brow furrowed ever so slightly.

"Mommie, are you sure she's ours?"

Camille was caught off guard. "Why?" she asked.

"Cause she looks like old Mr. Raskin from across the street."

Camille laughed. "Actually, sweetheart, she looks just like you did when you were born...just smaller."

Casey looked at her mother in horror, then back at the baby.

Shaking her head, she uttered emphatically, "Uh,u-u-uh!!"

***

Not far from the nursery, just down the hall to the right, was Dr. Hyer's office. Casey soon found herself deposited in the doctor's outer office, perched on a big, wooden chair, waiting for her mother. She glanced around, sizing up her surroundings. She stared curiously at the two women and a man who sat silently in the other wooden chairs, also waiting. For what, she didn't know. A nurse in a starched-white uniform was stationed behind a sliding glass window doing paperwork of some kind. The only noise in the room was the slight ticking of the clock on the wall. Casey was beginning to feel her senses dull.

She looked around the small room hoping to find something to distract herself. There was not a lot for a kid to do, especially when she found herself completely surrounded by adults. But, the matter was clearly out of her hands. So, there she waited -- for who knows how long, she thought -- as she began impatiently swinging one of her legs back and forth like an erratic pendulum.

**

Inside the doctor's office, Camille was anxious to get an update on her and the baby's condition from old Doc Hyer. Sitting behind his big oak desk, Dr. Hyer was conscientiously looking through a file that he had laying flat on his desk. He looked up for a moment and peered over the rims of his bifocals at Camille as she sat there before him. He smiled reassuringly and then went back to reading his file. Camille waited patiently for him to finish.

Being that he was Cedar Grove's only doctor, folks around town expected Doc Hyer to know a little about a whole lot of things. Through the years, he had managed to garner their confidence. His grandfatherly appearance put folks at ease. Something about the way his small pot belly protruded from underneath his tufted, paisley vest seemed to imbue him with an easy going, trustworthy manner.

Having finished reviewing the file, he removed his bifocals and placed them on the desk in front of him. He looked at Camille and spoke in a calm and reassuring tone.

"That steering wheel would have done you considerably more damage if the baby hadn't taken some of the blow," he informed her. "But, I don't think there's a problem of you having more children."

Camille's eyebrows raised skyward at his comment. "Frankly, Doctor, the two I have will do me just fine."

The doctor nodded and continued with his prognosis, "It is impossible to determine the extent of the baby's..."

Camille quickly interjected, "Call her Lillian. Lilly...for short."

The doctor nodded again and continued, "As I was sayin', it is impossible to determine the full extent of 'Lilly's' injuries. She suffered a fairly massive bruise in her temporal region. There could be complications later on."

Complications? Camille's mind began to whirl. This was clearly not the kind of thing she was prepared to hear. "What are you sayin'? she asked. "You sayin' she's got more than just a bump on the head?"

"Maybe," he said calmly, trying not to alarm her. "If she did suffer any brain damage..."

Camille was stunned, "Brain damage?!"

"I said, if. If she did suffer any, then it may not be evident for some time."

"Then you're really not sure?" she asked anxiously.

"No. The truth is, there's no way we can be absolutely certain, at least not right now."

"There must be something I can do," she said hopefully, "to make it better."

"Not really," he answered, "we're just going to have to wait." He paused, then offered his best advice. "I suggest you treat her...'Lillian'...like any other child. There's a good possibility she'll mend and be as normal as Cassandra."

***

Outside in Doc Hyer's waiting room, the aforementioned Cassandra had managed to amuse herself and stave off the tedium of the moment by making weird faces at a large man reading a magazine. Sensing an intrusive presence, the man quickly looked up and directly at her. Much to Casey's delight, he didn't catch her. As the man, once again, retreated to the privacy of his magazine, a frustrated Casey sat back and sighed -- bored stiff.

2)   FAMILY MATTERS

From that day forward, their lives were never the same. Time would soon disclose that even the most innocent among them could not come into this world without risks. It wasn't until several years later that they found out the real truth about what happened to Lilly that night in the rain and darkness. The more she grew, the more it was revealed to them.

A full three years later, a beaten up old Hudson with its front fender still crunched up under the hood drove slowly through a modest, slightly rundown neighborhood. The old car pulled into the driveway of a small house that was in need of a good coat of paint. As the car came to a stop, an active nine-year-old hopped out of the passenger's side and quickly closed the big, heavy door behind her. Her mother climbed out of the driver's side of the car and called out to her.

"Casey, honey, please take Lilly into the house for me while I get the groceries."

Camille reached back into the car and pulled a pretty and perky, perfectly normal looking, little three-year-old from the center of the seat to behind the steering wheel, so Casey could get to her. The small child didn't hesitate to slide behind the wheel, gripping it in her tiny hands.

As Casey skipped around the front of the car to retrieve her little sister from the front seat, Lilly was busy steering away pretending to be driving.

"Mommie, Lilly's going for another ride," Casey joked.

"Honey, just get her out of there, will you please, we've got a lot to get done," instructed her mother.

Casey dutifully took Lilly by the hand, pulling her out from behind the wheel and out of the car, as her mother hauled a bag of groceries from the back seat of the old Hudson. Lilly had become a beautiful, angelic-looking child with blond gossamer ringlets that framed her sweetly innocent face. She stared up at Casey expectantly with big trusting eyes.

Casey spoke to her as if sharing a secret, "Mama's gonna bake some pies for the church. She says if we're real good, she'll let us have some."

Casey, herself, was practically drooling. She rapidly shook her head "yes" as she gleefully gave Lilly a big, silly "um-ummm" smile. Lilly looked at Casey. She bobbed her head up and down as she mimicked her big sister. Tickled at the response, Casey beamed at her little sister's reaction. "Yeah...that's right, Lilly. Cho-co-late pie!"

"Girls," their mother interrupted, "get in the house. We don't have all day." Camille heaved a second bag of groceries onto her slender right hip. "Casey, take your sister to the bathroom," she ordered.

Casey looked at Lilly. "You hear that, Lilly? Mama said, 'we don't have all day.'" With that, Casey grabbed Lilly from around the back, hoisted her feet off of the ground and lugged her up the steps into the house.

***

A short time later, inside their modest house, Casey's Mom had laid out all of the ingredients needed to bake the pies. Eggs, sugar, milk, vanilla, cocoa, lemons and an assortment of other temptations covered the kitchen table. The table took up the bulk of the space just outside their cramped, little kitchen. The kitchen itself provided just enough room for a stove, a sink, an old ice box and about two feet of counter space.

There were, by far, fancier kitchens, but none more immaculately kept. Not a crumb could be found anywhere. The few square feet that composed the tiny tile floor gleamed with a fresh wax shine that had been diligently applied. Much like the orderly assortment of pie ingredients that had been so carefully set out on the table, everything in the small kitchen had been neatly appropriated to its proper place.

12

The same could be said about Lilly as she sat in her high chair, positioned next to the table, as Casey played Jacks nearby. Camille had just finished sprinkling her pie plates with a light dusting of flour when the jangling of the phone in the hallway interrupted their serene setting. Camille briskly dusted the flour residue off of her hands onto her terrycloth apron and then stepped over Casey to go and answer it.

"Keep an eye on your sister," she ordered. Casey nodded agreeably as her mother headed for the small hallway just off the living room.

Camille lifted the phone receiver to her ear and said, "Hello." As soon as she heard the voice on the other end of the line, her body stiffened. Standing perfectly still, with her back straight and shoulders erect, she suddenly found herself standing at attention.

"Well, yes, Mrs. Creighton. Yes, of course. You needn't worry," she said into the phone. "You can count on me. I promise. I'll have the pies there in time for the picnic."

Camille continued to listen attentively. As she was about to say something, she was distracted by an odd "plopping" sound. Just as quickly as it had begun, however, it stopped. Dismissing it, Camille continued talking, "No, no. I don't have any money left over from the church funds. I had to spend all that you gave me on the ingredients."

Once again, her thoughts were interrupted by a strange "plop... plop ... plop." Curious but still uncertain as to what it was, she hesitated...but again continued her conversation, "As you know, you pay a pretty penny for cocoa, butter and EGGS... oh..." Her eyes widened, "...uhhh, these days," she stammered. "Mrs. Creighton, I have to go. My, uh, my oven's heating up." Panicked, she dropped the phone and dashed back into the small dining area.

***

There was no mistaking it, the sight she had feared the most. Having crawled out of her high chair, there sat Lilly, smack in

13

the middle of the table, surrounded on all sides by raw eggs and cracked shells. Lilly beamed up at her mother as she gleefully held an *egg* in each of her small hands.

Aghast at the sight, Camille yelled out, "NO...Lilly!!"

Unfazed by her mother's anguished cries, Lilly giggled and gleefully tossed each of her oval missiles into the goop around her...plop, plop.

Camille's cries of anguish suddenly turned to anger.

"Cassandra Elizabeth Castle!" she screamed.

Wild eyed and panicked, Casey dashed into room. She saw the fury in her mother's eyes. She then looked up and saw Lilly perched in the middle of the scrambled mess.

"Oh, man...Lilly."

As Lilly made a play for more eggs, Casey and her mom dashed to the table.

Casey grabbed the few remaining eggs out of her reach as her mother lifted Lilly off the table. The thick, gooey mixture of yokes and whites dripped off of Lilly's dress down onto the table below. Camille looked at Casey, exasperated.

"You clean this up right now, young lady, while I try to keep your sister from turning into a soufflé. I am very upset with you, Cassandra.

Whoa. Cassandra. Not a good sign, not a good sign at all, thought Casey to herself. This was real trouble. Her mind started moving a mile a minute. She stared up at her mother hoping for leniency.

"Mom, I'm sorry," she said, woefully, "I just went to get a funny book."

"Did I or did I not ask you to watch your sister?!" Camille's face turned bright red. Her expression was a combination of anguish mixed with anger. She was clearly too distraught to show any mercy. Before Casey could squeak out her answer, she was quickly brushed aside.

"I don't want to hear it," her mother yelled. "All I want is to see this mess cleaned up by the time I get back in here." She picked up a dish towel and shoved it into Casey's hands. Again, looking at the table, Camille shook her head, "Look at this mess! I barely have enough eggs to finish the pies!"

Distraught, she whisked Lilly away.

Casey stared at the daunting task before her. She grimaced as she began to clean up the messy glop. Swirling the small dish towel around in the middle of the sticky, yellow eggs and shells only seemed to make matters worse. She gagged and felt nauseous as the thick, gooey mess clung to the dish towel. The more she wiped, the more she seemed to smear its collagenous streaks across the table.

She grimaced to herself, "Yuck, yuck...double yuck."

***

Fortunately by the next morning, following a good night's sleep, nerves had calmed and things had settled down nicely. It was a beautiful Sunday morning and the pie incident was all but forgotten. Dressed in their best cotton dresses for their trip to the church, Camille piled the two girls into the back seat of the old Hudson.

Propped up and sitting cross-legged in the big back seat, Casey pulled Lilly over next to her and opened the pages of her comic book. Enjoying the attention, Lilly stared down at the pictures as Casey began reading -- "Daffy said, 'What do you know about it? You're just a dumb rabbit.'"

With the girls comfortably settled in, their mom rushed back into the house and began to bring out the pies. She placed three on the car's front seat and two on the floor below. As she stared down at the sumptuous looking pies, she felt contented. She was quite certain that Betty Crocker herself couldn't have done a better job. She looked into the back seat at her two daughters and smiled.

"Well, at least we saved half of them." Satisfied, she closed the car door.

Suddenly, she heard the phone ringing inside the house. Poking her head through the open car window, she quickly ordered, "Don't move, I'll be right back."

Moments later, on the phone, Camille grimaced slightly as she listened. Shifting impatiently from one foot to the other, she finally managed to blurt out, "Yes, Mrs. Creighton, they came out just fine. We're on our way." Again, she found herself listening. "All right. All right. All...right," she replied, doing her best to remain calm. "Yes, well then, good..." All she could hear was a dial tone in her ear before she even had a chance to say "good-bye."

Nonplused, Camille hung up the phone and shook her head in disgust. Sighing deeply, she glanced upward, "I know, Lord, I shouldn't be having such thoughts on your day."

With Mrs. Creighton out of her hair and without further delay, Camille was once more out the door, heading for the car. All things considered, her efforts had turned out fairly well. All that was left was a quick drive to the church.

As she approached the car, her heart skipped a beat. She stopped cold in her tracks. She saw it, but she could not believe it. Lilly was standing in the middle of the front seat. Numbed, Camille could barely move her body forward to see what her brain was already telling her. As she neared the car, her worst fears were realized. Lilly was standing there with her right foot in one of the pies and her left foot in another. Her hands and dress were covered with coconut meringue, chocolate and lemon. Totally unaware of the calamity that had befallen her, Casey was happily buried, nose deep into her comic book in the back seat. Just as she was just about to turn the page, she was rudely shaken to the core of her very being. "Startled witless" by a loud, screeching howl -- Casey looked up in horror. Much to her surprise, it was her mother.

"Lilly! Casey! Oh, my God!"

Casey bolted up from the back seat in a panic. Before her was a disastrous sight -- her little sister covered from head to toe with the remnants of her mother's pies. Her body went limp. Then to further the horror, stark terror crossed her face as her comic book began tumbling involuntarily -- as if in slow motion -- out of her numbed hands. Set on an irretrievable course, it became like a missile picking up speed. Plunging downward, its direction unaltered, Casey watched as it landed smack in the middle of one of the previously undisturbed chocolate pies.

Petrified, she couldn't speak. She sat back quickly, motionless, mouth open and stared upward into her mother's glaring face.

Her mom's words had a surreal echo to them. "Can't I leave you alone for a minute?" shrieked her mother. "Do you have any idea what you've done!?"

Casey's shock paralyzed her body. Stunned, she watched her mother in total exasperation grab the chocolate laden comic book out of the pie and start ripping it...and ripping it...to shreds. Casey was clearly beyond speechless as the shredded pages of the comic book flittered down to the ground around her mother's feet. She got out of the car not knowing what to do.

Then, just as suddenly as it had begun, she saw her mother's anger turn to tears. Overwhelmed, Camille walked back to the house and collapsed on the front steps. Holding her head in her hands, she began to sob.

Mortified, Casey huddled up against the car door and watched as the tears streamed down her mother's face. She could not bear the sight. Her mother's desperation seemed to wrench her very soul. Feeling helpless to do anything, she looked inside the car at the mess. It only exacerbated her guilt. She took a deep breath, reached over for Lilly's hand and pulled her out of the car.

Still seated on the porch, Camille finally managed to calm herself and stop crying. As she wiped her face and looked up, she saw Casey coming up the walk hand-in-hand with her little sister. They looked like two bygone waifs abandoned in a storm. Camille took one look at Casey's drooping, hang-dog face and Lilly's chocolate-coconut-lemon flavored little body and began to shake.

Unable to control herself, she suddenly broke into gales of bellowing laughter. Casey walked over next to her, bewildered at her mother's unusual reaction.

"Mommie, I'm sorry. She's so fast. I didn't see her."

Before Camille could respond to Casey's heartfelt apology, little Lilly hopped into her mother's lap. Stunned, Camille looked at Lilly...then down at her own pie-covered dress. The light blue cotton print dress was now layered with a thin coating of pie and meringue. Once again, she roared with laughter as she rocked gleefully back and forth hugging her baby daughter. Concerned and confused, Casey stared at them both.

"Are you okay, Mommie?"

Camille stifled a laugh and then wiped some chocolate filling off of Lilly's chin with her finger and tasted it. Then, giggling uncontrollably, she gave her impartial critique, "H'mmm, not bad, if I say so myself."

Casey smiled at her, timidly, still unsure of her status.

"Mom, there's two on the floor she didn't get to. They still look real good," she said with a hopeful optimism.

Her mom reached over, pulled an uncertain Casey close and hugged her.

"Honey, I don't want you to give it another thought, okay? Listen, sweetie...they're just pies. You're my girls. And, nothing or nobody comes between me and my girls."

Still overwhelmed by guilt, Casey tried once again to explain herself. "I just looked away for a minute. I didn't see her."

Camille gently kissed her on the cheek, "I know, sweetie, it's hard."

"Mama, sometimes she moves so-o-o fast."

"She's like a little jackrabbit, isn't she?" Camille smiled and wrapped an arm snugly around Casey's waist. "Sweetheart, Lilly doesn't mean to cause trouble. She just doesn't know better. She's a special child." Casey listened carefully as her mother continued. "She's always going to need our love. And, she's always going to need us both to watch after her.

Sometimes, it's not going to be easy. So, what we'll do is the best we can, okay?"

Casey nodded. She didn't like letting her mom down. She would do her best to help, she thought to herself.

***

Across town at the Church of Cedar Grove, the church auditorium buzzed with activity as church women moved about assembling their various dishes on long tables that had been set up for the indoor-outdoor picnic. After last year's outing, some of the older ladies concluded that they would be considerably more comfortable dining inside out of the scorching heat of the afternoon sun. Hence, an indoor-outdoor motif was born out of an afternoon of moist décolletages. That was not to say that several wouldn't chance to venture out later after the meal to observe a hearty game of softball. A rare, but possible, occurrence should the conversation inside fail to include the necessary highlights to harbor their attention.

But, at that moment, preparations were at hand. Children of all sizes scurried about, mostly under foot, as large platters and basting tins of pork ribs, chicken and biscuits were being carried into the kitchen at the back of the large auditorium. In a matter of hours, the entrees would be grilled, fried and baked into a veritable feast for all comers.

Emerging from among the clamor, was one of Cedar Grove's leading ladies, Mrs. Eleanor Hotchkiss Creighton. Politely described as a sizable woman, she frequently defied conventional fashion for a person of her stature. She was unabashedly decked out in a white, silk dress with large, red flowers that appeared to be blossoming in festive array about her full figured frame. Nose held high, she had the air of a no-nonsense commandant as she surveyed the activity in the auditorium.

It was her opinion that somebody had to set the standard, even in a small town like Cedar Grove. Mrs. Creighton had long ago elevated herself to the lofty position of civic overseer. Qualifications were essentially based on income and attitude.

She had both.

Flung across one of her ample hips, dressed in his blue and white sailor's suit, was her two-year-old grandson, Leonard. As Mrs. Creighton approached a row of long tables that were covered with side dishes, she deftly swung Leonard off her hip and stood the child on one of the table tops. She then picked up a plastic fork and sampled from a large bowl of potato salad.

As Mrs. Creighton plunged the fork through the salad's colorful top layer of relish and pimentos, Edna, a sweet looking older woman who had made the salad, became distracted by Mrs. Creighton's grandchild. Pinching his plump little cheeks, Edna began to coo at the small child, "Ooo, what a beautiful grandbaby. Hel-wo, sweetie."

Mrs. Creighton bit down on the salad. Her mouth puckered ever so slightly. With the artistry of a street magician -- she quickly feigned a cough, grabbed a napkin, covered her mouth and ejected the sample with a fake sneeze.

Smiling sweetly, she tossed the expectorated sample into a trash can under the table and said, "Edna, dear, as usual, your potato salad is beyond description."

As Edna was about to express her appreciation, Mrs. Creighton's grandson made a play and reached for the potato salad. Mrs. Creighton quickly grabbed the toddler's hand. "No, no dear, you don't want that."

Across the room, a distance from the two women, towns people continued to stream through the front doors of the auditorium. Some were carrying folding chairs, others were bringing in more food.

Among them, freshly scrubbed and without a speck of chocolate or meringue on them, were Camille, Casey and Lilly. Camille was carrying the two surviving pies from the Lilly disaster. She carefully put them down on the table beside Mrs. Creighton and Edna.

Edna looked at her sympathetically, "Camille, I heard about the pies. What a dreadful thing to have happen after all that work."

Mrs. Creighton's tone was far less sympathetic, "Yes, yes, Mrs. Castle, what a pity," she droned. "Being a waitress, I would have thought you'd be far more adept at handling food."

"Accidents happen, Mrs. Creighton," said Camille, unfazed.

"But, my dear, two pies are hardly worth all the money we doled out to you," lamented Mrs. Creighton. Then, with an accusatory look, "Assuming, of course, you actually 'bought' enough ingredients to make more than two pies." Mrs. Creighton had suddenly metamorphosed from civic overseer to self-proclaimed prosecutor.

Incensed at such a clearly unsubstantiated accusation, Camille immediately became indignant, "I can assure you," she stammered, "after Lilly's first accident, I used every bit of the ingredients to bake those pies!"

Mrs. Creighton practically sneered, "Yes, well, that's something I would have liked to have seen for myself. Besides, pray tell," she said rolling her eyes upwards, "how many 'accidents' can one child have?"

Camille fought to control herself. "Mrs. Creighton," she said firmly, "Lilly didn't know any better. And, she certainly didn't know they were meant for the church. To her, they were just pies."

Mrs. Creighton looked at Lilly then back at Camille. "Of course, you're right, dear," she said. "I suppose you have to expect those kinds of things will happen when you have a child with a mental defect."

No sooner had Mrs. Creighton mouthed the derisive remark, than she heard a distinct squishing sound. The women all turned around to see Mrs. Creighton's grandson with his hands and knees firmly planted in the middle of Camille's two remaining pies.

Mrs. Creighton was horrified, "Leonard!" Startled, the child suddenly ended up, *bottoms down*, in the middle of one of the pie plates.

Camille was barely able to restrain her giggles, "I'm sorry, Mrs. Creighton, you were saying...?"

Trying hard not to snicker out loud, Edna covered her mouth with both of her hands as Mrs. Creighton lifted her grandson out of the gooey mess. Camille fought to subdue her own laughter as she politely nodded to the two women.

"Edna, Mrs. Creighton...Leonard," she said, still struggling to maintain a little decorum. Camille reached down, picked up Lilly and took Casey by the hand. She and the girls turned and walked out of the church auditorium. Smiling to herself, she glanced upward, "Thank you, Lord. You truly do work in mysterious ways."

***

The little family exited the building and walked hand-in-hand down the front steps. Having escaped -- virtually unscathed -- from the encounter with the mighty Mrs. Creighton, Casey could sense her mother's ease.

As the three of them reached the bottom of the steps, Casey saw two little girls about her age, coming her way. They were laughing and smiling as they tightly held the hands of a man Casey assumed to be their father. She was struck how handsome he looked in his light blue coat and dark blue tie as the girls danced around him in their matching daisy-print dresses. They surely were dressed up nice for a picnic, she thought to herself.

She stared in wonderment as they drew closer to her. She could see the man's apparent joy as he delighted in spending time with his two little girls. She watched his gentleness with them as they skipped around him so happy and carefree. Mesmerized by the big, broad smile on their dad's face, Casey allowed herself, for a brief instant, to be transported into their happiness. Her mind wondering, she could only imagine what it would be like.

And then, like a bolt out of the blue, it hit her -- a sharp pang of envy. A gnawing ache seemed to suddenly overwhelm her. Deep in the recesses of her mind, she could feel the jabbing sting of a painful memory -- one that she could never seem to completely erase. Her heart sank in her chest. She quickly looked away. Some things were better left forgotten. Still, she couldn't help but take one last look and wonder.

Seeing the plaintive look on Casey's face, her mom stared at her curiously.

"Honey," she said, "you okay?"

Jolted from her mental meandering, Casey looked up at her mom. She could see her sweet look of concern. It was a comforting sight. In Casey's eyes, her mother looked beautiful in her plain cotton dress with her hair slightly tousled and collar askew from little Lilly's wandering hands.

Proudly, Casey grasped her mom's hand tightly in her own, took a deep breath and smiled. "Yeah, Mama, it's nothin'. I'm fine."

3)   LIFE & OTHER SLIPPERY SLOPES

It was no easy task for a woman alone to raise a family, especially in a small town. It wasn't that Cedar Grove was any more or less forgiving than anywhere else. Though, admittedly, some folks had a tendency to hold a single mother without a man somewhat suspect. Camille, of course, didn't have time to be bothered with what other people perceived as her shortcomings. Man or no man, she had two mouths to feed.

It was late in the day and Camille was away at work. She had left the two girls in the very capable hands of Mrs. Eberworth, the next door neighbor. Mrs. Eberworth was a well-rounded, older lady who liked to say that her people had come from the land. Her soft-pin-cushion-ey, grandmotherly look was accentuated by her graying reddish-hair that sat neatly wrapped atop her head like a cinnamon bun. Outward appearances, however, far from told her story. Underneath her gentle exterior, was a backbone of tempered steel and there was no doubt that she knew a thing or two about caring for two young girls. Having raised her own family and now widowed, she had been a help to Camille for as long as anybody could remember. Camille had often said, she'd be lost without her. And, so it was again.

The house was quiet as Mrs. Eberworth carried a very drowsy Lilly up the stairs. Casey led the way and opened the door to her mother's bedroom.

As Mrs. Eberworth gently placed Lilly onto the double bed, Casey leaned over and kissed Lilly on the cheek. Lilly's nose crinkled slightly and Casey chuckled to herself. Thinking it was funny, she leaned down and gave Lilly another light kiss. Once more, Lilly crinkled her nose at the unknown irritation.

"Honey, leave her be," cautioned Mrs. Eberworth. "Don't wake her up."

Casey nodded and quietly stepped away from the bed.

Mrs. Eberworth looked around the room and saw an old window air conditioner sticking out of the lower window next to the bed. She went over to it and started fidgeting with its knobs. She pushed the "ON" switch. Nothing happened. Seeing the temperature gage, she gave it a good turn. Still, nothing happened. She stared at the brown box as it sat silently there in the window. Perplexed, she looked down at Casey.

"How the heck does this thing work?" she asked.

"It doesn't," Casey piped up. "Mama says it's just for show."

"Well, sweetie, why didn't you tell me that in the first place?"

"Thought maybe you could fix it. Mama says you can fix pretty near anything."

Mrs. Eberworth looked back at the old, brown air conditioner.

"This thing is way beyond my help. I'm afraid it's a goner."

"Yup, Mama figures it 'died a sure death' some time ago."

"Don't matter," shrugged Mrs. Eberworth as she decided on another plan of action. "I'll just open the top window. Fresh air will do her better anyway."

Casey nodded in agreement. As Mrs. Eberworth opened the window above the old air conditioner, a light breeze rustled through the thin, white curtains. Satisfied, she looked over at Casey and whispered, "All right, let's go finish up."

Casey and Mrs. Eberworth quietly slipped out of the room, leaving a peacefully sleeping Lilly.

***

Downstairs, Casey and Mrs. Eberworth each had a large bowl placed directly in front of them as they sat around the small kitchen table preparing to snap beans. A pile of fresh green beans was stacked in the center of the small table. Another empty bowl was positioned between them.

"Now, this bowl here stays between us. It's for the beans that don't make the cut," explained Mrs. Eberworth. "Those are the ones we gotta weed out."

"How come?" asked Casey.

Mrs. Eberworth plucked a shriveled, brownish bean out of the green pile in front of them. "All right, now you see how green and firm most of 'em are?"

"Uh-huh," answered an attentive Casey.

"Well, them's that's not, like this one here, goes into the extra bowl. Got it?"

"Got it," responded Casey.

Casey watched Mrs. Eberworth snap some of the fresh green beans into smaller pieces and drop them into the bowl in front of her. Casey then took her own handful and began snapping them, copying Mrs. Eberworth's every move.

After a few seconds, Casey looked up at Mrs. Eberworth, inquisitively. "Mrs. Eberworth, what are you gonna do with these beans?"

"I'm gonna cook 'em up and give half to your mama and keep half for my supper."

The answer suited Casey just fine. She liked Mrs. Eberworth.

"Mrs. Eberworth...?"

Without looking up from her bowl of beans Mrs. Eberworth answered, "Yes, dear."

"Mama said you've known us since before I was born."

"Well, your mama would be right about that," said Mrs. Eberworth.

"You must of known my daddy then?" Casey stopped snapping her beans and looked over at her for the answer.

"Can't really say I did. Your dad more or less kept to himself. It was his way."

Casey paused for a moment, then said, "I heard him tell my mama that we was livin' on the backside of nowhere, that we didn't even belong to him."

Mrs. Eberworth kept on snapping her beans. "Sometimes, Casey, people say things they don't really mean. Especially when they're angry."

Casey was astounded. "Was he mad at us?"

Mrs. Eberworth looked at her, then said calmly, "No, honey, he was mad at the world. That's the way it is with some people," she added.

Mrs. Eberworth stopped snapping her beans. "Casey, honey, the thing is...sometimes life deals out a bad hand. I'm not sayin' it's fair, I'm just sayin' it happens to most everybody at some time or another. The trick is how you handle it. Just remember this one thing...regardless of the circumstances, what a body has to do, child -- is to get over it and get on with it -- whether it takes several years or just one day at a time. That's what your mama did."

Casey was satisfied with Mrs. Eberworth's forthrightness. She liked how she talked to her straight out. Still, she had other things on her mind.

"Mrs. Eberworth?"

"Yes, dear," she said, resuming her bean snapping.

"Do you think Lilly will ever talk?"

"Can't rightly say."

"I tried to teach her hopscotch. She just stood there, wouldn't do anything. I heard people say she's dumb."

Mrs. Eberworth bristled slightly, "If they let you hear that, then they're the ones that's dumb." She stopped snapping her beans and looked at Casey. "Best I know, little one, it's like parts of Lilly's brain is workin' and other parts aren't... 'cause of the accident. She understands some stuff, but other stuff is just too hard for her to follow. But, one thing's for certain, she is one precious, lovin' child. And that, my darlin', among all that life gives us...is a gift from God."

Suddenly the screen door to the kitchen opened and Camille came in. She was wearing her waitress uniform. It was obvious she had had a rough day. Looking a little frayed around the edges, several wayward strands of her hair dangled down from what had started out earlier in the day as a very smart French twist. Casey beamed at her mother. "Mama!"

"Hi, doll. Hello, Mrs. Eberworth. How's it going?"

"Oh, fair to midlin'", said Mrs. Eberworth. "Yourself?"

"Been better. Car broke down. Jessie's husband towed it to the shop, then gave me a ride home." Camille sighed and looked around. "Where's Lilly?"

"Upstairs in your bed resting like the little angel she is."

Camille smiled, then leaned down and kissed Casey on the cheek. "Have you been a big help to Mrs. Eberworth?"

Casey proudly showed off her half-filled bowl of beans.

Mrs. Eberworth beamed at Casey. "Been teachin' this child everything I know about the finer art of bean snapping."

"Well, I thank you both," Camille said looking over the beans, "I expect these are gonna be mighty tasty."

Suddenly, there was a thunk from outside of the house. Camille was momentarily distracted by the sound, but quickly dismissed it as Mrs. Eberworth diverted her attention. "I was thinking, Camille, why don't I just cook up this whole batch. Won't be any extra trouble."

Camille was delighted, "That would be wonderful. Last time I ate your fresh snapped beans I thought I'd died and gone to heaven." This pleased Mrs. Eberworth.

As Camille started towards the stairs, she looked back teasing, "If you two 'whipper-<u>snappers</u>' will excuse me, I think I'll go up and check on Lilly."

"Mom..." Casey rolled her eyes upward, "that was really corny."

Mrs. Eberworth immediately took umbrage, "Well, now, not so fast, youngin'. It's my experience...a little corn always makes a fine addition to a menu."

Casey groaned, loudly. Camille laughed and went up the stairs.

***

Moments later, in her bedroom, Camille looked around. Much to her surprise, she didn't see Lilly lying on the bed as she had expected. In fact, she didn't see Lilly anywhere. She called out for her as she looked under and on both sides of the bed.

"Lilly, baby, Mommie's home. Lilly?" Then, a little more anxiously, "Honey, where are you?"

She looked out into the small hallway and could clearly see that both of the doors to the bathroom and to the girls' bedroom were completely shut. Dismayed, she went back into her room and looked around.

She stood there, baffled. As she looked around again, the open window above the air conditioner caught her attention. Her heart practically stopped. She quickly rushed to the window. For several frightening moments, she peered out of the window, down through the branches of a tree, to the ground below. Lilly was nowhere in sight. Relieved, she rushed back downstairs to the kitchen.

"Lilly's not in the bedroom. Did she come down here?" she asked.

Surprised, Casey and Mrs. Eberworth looked at each other and shook their heads. As Casey was about to speak, they heard a barely audible sound coming from outside the kitchen's screen door.

"Mom-mie."

In disbelief, all three remained perfectly still, as if frozen in place. Once again the weak, little voice called out, "Mom-mie." Camille's face blanched white as she rushed to the screen door. There was Lilly.

She was trying to climb up the steps towards the back door. Struggling with all of her might to keep her balance, she placed her little hands as firmly as she could, palms down, on the back steps. There were scratches all over her arms and face and she was having trouble breathing.

Stunned at the sight of her baby daughter, Camille hurriedly opened the screen door and picked up her child. "Oh, my baby. My sweet baby."

Lilly gasped for breath.

Mrs. Eberworth was mortified, "Oh, Lord. She's turning blue."

Camille looked down at Lilly as she held her in her arms. "Oh, my God, oh my God, she can't breath." Camille screamed in panic, "I've got to get her to the hospital."

Mrs. Eberworth started towards the hall phone, "I'll call an ambulance."

Camille yelled after her, "There's no time!"

"But, you don't have your car," Mrs. Eberworth anxiously reminded her.

"The county hospital is just around the block." Camille yelled to her, "Please, call them! Tell them I'm bringing her in."

Near panic, Camille desperately ran out of the back door, clutching her child in her arms. Casey started to bolt after her, tears welling in her eyes. Mrs. Eberworth reached out to grab her. She was barely able to catch Casey by the arm, holding her back.

"No, honey, this is something your mama has to do by herself."

Frightened, Casey clung to Mrs. Eberworth as tears streamed silently down her face. It was not the first time she had seen her family in jeopardy.

***

Several terrifying minutes later, Camille made her way to the emergency entrance at Cedar Grove Hospital. The emergency room was fairly quiet as Camille rushed through the back door...desperate and in tears.

"Help me!" she screamed. "My baby can't breath. Somebody help me!"

She barely finished her plea for help when a rather stout, older nurse forcefully whisked Lilly out of Camille's arms and barked an order at the reception clerk. "Get the doctor down here...now!"

The nurse brushed Camille aside, placed Lilly on a gurney and began CPR.

Lilly was blue. She was not moving.

4)   HEARTS BROKEN

Like all towns, big and small, crises and emergencies come and go. Then, life goes on -- except, of course, for the people directly affected by them. Two weeks had passed and life in Cedar Grove could best be described as status quo.

Even at Casey's house, nothing out of the ordinary appeared to be going on...at least, not on the surface. From general appearances, it was just another bright, Summer's day. The only thing that might be considered vaguely out of order was a strange car that was parked out in front at the end of the sidewalk. Having been banished by her mother to play outside, Casey was examining the car with a great curiosity. Catching a glimpse of her own reflection, she struck her most captivating pose as she admired herself in one of the car's side mirrors.

***

Inside Casey's house, a woman and a man were sitting stiffly on a small sofa that took up the better part of the what Camille liked to refer to as the living room. The two appeared to be uncomfortable and cramped even though they sat the full distance of the sofa away from each other. Both were dressed in drab brown and their dour expressions gave them the appearance of low level bureaucrats on a bad day. They were there for a purpose and it was evident they were uneasy at best with the task at hand.

Impatient to conclude their visit, the woman nervously pulled at some of the rose-colored threads that had broken loose from the sofa's frayed piping. She methodically wrapped the fragile threads around her index finger.

Sitting before them, alone and defenseless, was Camille. She was silent as she dabbed her red, swollen eyes with a handkerchief. The man spoke as sympathetically and as gently as he could to her, "Mrs. Castle, the accident was a sign. All things considered, you're very fortunate that Lilly only had the wind knocked out of her along with..."

"Along with bruised ribs and scratches!!" bristled the woman, interrupting. "Why, that child could have been killed!" she declared, as she snapped one of the thin threads off the arm of the sofa.

The man turned and glared at the woman, then continued speaking in a very gentle voice to Camille. "Obviously, it could have been much worse."

Camille almost seemed *broken* as the man continued. "Putting her in a state school is for her protection. It is impossible for two parents...much less a single, working mother...to take proper care of a child like Lilly."

Camille broke down in tears, "But she's my baby."

Undeterred, he continued, "Mrs. Castle, mentally retarded children can be a real hardship."

"He's right," insisted the woman. "Most parents prefer to put them in a state run school. Besides," she continued, "living in an institution is really not such a bad thing, especially for these kind of children."

Camille looked up at the woman, bitterly. "Really? Then why don't you tell me that after you've lived in one!"

The man, Mr. Wiggins, could see her pain. With as much compassion as possible, he once more spoke to Camille.

"Mrs. Castle, you are not abandoning her. You have to understand, it really is in the best interest of the child."

Camille choked back the tears, barely able to speak.

"Is it, Mr. Wiggins?"

"Yes ma'am...it is."

Overwhelmed by feelings of hopelessness, it was a moment frozen in time for Camille as she stared at the two strangers -- unable to respond.

***

34

Not unlike a volcano, some people's lives seem to have one eruption after another. And, so it was for Casey and her mom. Once again, in her innocence, Lilly brought about a series of events that reshaped their world as they knew it. Try as they would, there was not one thing they could do about it. It had been a month since the visit from the state school people and the days became more and more precious for the small family as each week went by.

Uppermost in Casey's mind, was the limited time she had left. There was much to do and not much time to do it. She was determined to spend as much time with Lilly as possible. One evening, several weeks later, it was still early as Casey and Lilly sat on the bed in their pajamas. Casey was doing her best to get Lilly to pay attention.

"Lilly...you said it. You said, 'mommie!' That means you can talk," she insisted. "Now look," she continued, "Mama says, they're gonna take you away 'cause you can't talk. So, this is real important, okay?"

Casey took a deep breath and tried again.

"Okay. Say, my name is Lilly." Casey repeated it slowly, "My...name...is...Lilly."

Lilly just smiled at her. Frustrated, Casey looked at Lilly earnestly.

"C'mon, Lilly, you're not trying. You can't go to some dumb 'ol school. You gotta stay here with us. Mama says, we're a family."

Bored with the game, Lilly snuggled down on the bed and nestled up to her pillow. Casey looked at her, haplessly. Realizing she was not going to get Lilly to budge, she pulled a light blanket over her.

"Gettin' sleepy, huh? Okay, we'll try again tomorrow. But remember, we don't have a whole lot of time."

Lilly beamed up at her with one of her mischievous smiles and suddenly started kicking the blanket off. Casey perked up. She knew this game.

"Oh! I see. So, you're not too sleepy to play, huh?"

Lilly gave the blanket another swift kick. Casey pretended surprise and started to make her move. "Yeah...well, you better watch out 'cause I'm gonna GET YOU!"

With that, Casey started tickling her little sister, unmercifully. As Lilly tried to wriggle out of Casey's reach, she let out screams of laughter, enjoying every minute of it. Just as Casey was ready to move in for another attack, the bedroom door swung open. Their mother popped her head in.

"Enough you two. It's time to go to sleep," she admonished. "Casey, honey, remember her ribs. You've got to be careful with her!"

Alarmed, Casey looked down at Lilly, "Oh...wow. I'm sorry."

Feeling no pain, Lilly looked back at her with glee and suddenly started kicking the blanket again ready to play some more.

"I don't know, Mom. She looks fine to me."

Camille went over to the bed, sat on the edge and began tucking her daughters in.

"You're a pair of little noodles, you know that?"

She pulled the covers up under their chins. "Now, sleep tight, don't let the alligators bite."

"Mom-mm...not alligators! *Bed bugs.*"

Camille looked at Casey with a teasing smile, "Oh, yeah. That's right...bed bugs. Alligators...have BIG TEETH!!" She raised her fingers high in the air and pretended they were big snapping teeth. The girls gleefully pulled up the covers and hid under them for protection. They laughed as she pulled the sheet away from their faces and kissed them both. She gave them one final tuck and smiled.

"Now, go to sleep."

As their mom headed for the door and turned out the light, she heard giggles coming from the darkened room.

"Girls."

More giggles were quickly followed by shushing sounds. The room was momentarily quiet. Then, in a soft whisper,

"I love you, Lilly."

In the darkened room, Casey reached over and took her little sister's hand in hers. "I've been thinkin'," she said quietly, "maybe if we ask God, he'll fix it so you don't have to go." Lilly shuffled around under the cover. Casey instructed her, "Okay now, be still. We gotta do this right. I'm not sure, but I think it'll be okay if I do all the talkin'."

Then in a quiet little voice, she offered up her prayer.

"Lord, this is Casey Castle speaking to you. I know you know us 'cause Mama says you do. It's about Lilly. Some people came to the house and want to take her away from us. But see, the thing is, Lord...Mama and me have been lookin' after her since she was born...and, maybe you noticed...we done a real good job. Well, at least Mama has. I guess you probably know I don't have much...but I'd give it all up if you would let her stay with us. I already lost my daddy. I don't think I could stand it if I lose Lilly, too. Please think on it, Lord. It'd really be important to me if you would. This is Casey Castle sayin' -- Amen."

***

A month later, a car was headed down a two lane highway that read Texas State Highway 290. As it proceeded about a mile farther, it passed by another sign that read: AUSTIN STATE SCHOOL FOR THE MENTALLY RETARDED.   It seemed the time had come. Camille was trying her best to remain firm and steady behind the wheel as she looked over at Lilly who was seated between her and Casey in the front seat. Both girls had been scrubbed to a "fare thee well" as Mrs. Eberworth was fond of saying and looked like two shiny pennies. Lilly always loved car trips, but the final destination for this one would bring no joy to anyone who was along for this long and difficult ride.

The car made a right turn, pulled off the highway and made its way down a road. Buildings seemed to appear out of the middle of nowhere. The car continued on, first passing by a brick administration building and then driving through several blocks of white, wooden buildings that looked like old army barracks. Casey stared out of the car window at the very unusual surroundings. Row after row of the sterile-looking white barracks gave the impression of housing some kind of government experiment. Casey had seen quonset hut-looking buildings just like them portrayed in many of the current day science fiction comic books.

She was relieved when they drove past a clinic. Ordinary looking people were walking to their cars and going about what looked like a normal day's business. Nothing odd about that. So far, so good -- she thought to herself.

Her mother drove the car up to the front of one of the white barracks with the number 77 on the entrance and stopped. Camille, Casey and Lilly got out of the car. Camille attentively smoothed down Lilly's neatly ironed dress and then began brushing her hair. Casey pulled a small suitcase, filled with Lilly's belongings, from the back seat.

As Casey set the suitcase down on the sidewalk, a very sweet looking black woman came out of the white barrack, smiled at down at Casey, picked up the suitcase and carried it inside.

Another woman passed by her and walked up to a now very unsteady Camille. The woman smiled warmly, "I'm Mrs. Womack. We've been expecting you."

Camille nodded. Her expression appeared hollow, as if she were in shock.

Mrs. Womack looked at Lilly, "This must be Lilly. What a beautiful child she is."

Camille smiled weakly down at Lilly and said, "Thank you."

Suddenly, a group of children about Lilly's age were being led from the white building. It was evident that they were all retarded, some severely. Casey looked at them. None of them looked like Lilly.

Unnerved, she looked at her little sister, then back at the children. The reality of Lilly's new existence suddenly hit her along with a pang of despair. Tears began to form. She quickly looked away. Her mind raced. This was not right. This could not be happening. She had to do something.

Frantically, she looked up at Mrs. Womack, "She can talk."

Mrs. Womack looked at her stunned, "What, dear?"

Desperate, Casey tried again.

"She can talk. She said, 'Mommie.'" Casey looked to her mother for help. "Tell her, Mama. Tell her she said it!"

Shaken by Casey's futile attempt to change the unchangeable, Camille stooped down and pulled her two daughters into her arms.

Casey began crying uncontrollably and pleaded, "Tell her, Mommie, tell her she said it."

As tears streamed down Camille's face, she pulled her daughters tightly to her. "Yes, sweetheart," she replied grief stricken, "she did. She said it."

With her heart bursting, Camille looked up, helplessly, at Mrs. Womack. Barely able to speak, she tried to assure her as the tears choked off her words, "She did...she really did say it."

Casey's sobs became uncontrollable as she realized the situation was beyond their control. Seeing her mother and sister in tears, little Lilly burst out crying -- unaware of the cause of their anguish.

Mrs. Womack watched as the small family of three held desperately to one another. There was nothing she could do. For that matter, there had never been anything she could do. For her, it was not an unfamiliar sight.

5) MAKING CHOICES

Though years passed, they never got used to Lilly being away, but they adjusted to it. As Casey grew older, it seemed strange to her how the world was so far out of sync with Lilly's innocence. Through no fault of her own, Lilly seemed to get caught up in events beyond anybody's control...and Casey and her mom got caught up with her. Not that Casey didn't already have enough to deal with on her own.

***

Cedar Grove High School was not a lot different from other small town high schools. It was the final day of school before summer break. Teenagers of all shapes and sizes filled its hallways, pushing and shoving their way out of post-puberty adolescence -- towards independence. A couple of guys, on a hormone high, whirled around to stare at a pretty seventeen-year-old as she made her way through the energetic mob.

She was a vision of blossoming femininity in her thin, cotton blouse -- its light, violet hue closely matching the color of her eyes. The two boys paid no attention to the frayed edges of her collar which appeared victim to one washing too many. Nor did they take notice of the worn-down heels of her finely polished penny loafers, both of which had extended well beyond normal life expectancy. All they knew is that they liked what they saw and a wolf whistle sent their message loud and clear. As she glanced their direction, they waved and grinned at her. Then, like the juveniles they were, they continued pushing and shoving each other as they made their way down the hallway. She smiled to herself, amused by their attention.

As she neared her locker, she reached back to free her shoulder-length, caramel-brown hair from its ponytail, allowing it to tumble down the back of her neck. She then opened the door to her locker. As she began to clear out the locker, she found herself suddenly being spun around and practically assaulted by her best friend, Mandy Banks, a feisty red-head with mischief on her mind.

"Casey!" Mandy yelled, excitedly.

Casey looked at her, startled, "Mandy, you almost gave me a heart attack."

"Get a load of this!" Mandy dangled a bright, yellow bikini in front of Casey, swinging it back and forth as if it were the two most tantalizing strips of cheap polyester on the planet.

Casey looked at her, "So, what about it?"

"It's a bikini, dufus."

"I know that, why'd you bring it to school?

"Bait."

"Bait?"

"Yeah," she said waving it again under Casey's nose. "For Eddie. I want him to see what he's gonna be missing if he goes off to California to see his dad. One look at me...in this...and that boy is mine for the summer."

Casey smirked, "A little far from the beach, aren't you, Annette?"

"Oh, please. Compared to this, that Funicello chick was wearin' a blanket."

Casey's eyebrows arched, "No argument there."

"I plan on taking Eddie to Cedar Creek this week-end, let him feast his eyes on this hot, little number," she said boldly, "and give him a preview of things to come."

"Mandy, you better slow down," Casey cautioned. "You're gonna end up getting more than you bargained for."

"Save it, Mom! I'm doin' whatever it takes to keep him here. I figure we've only got one more year of high school left and this is going to be my summer."

Casey knew that Mandy wasn't ditzy or a bona fide air head like some people thought. It was just that she was driven by one singular impulse that monopolized her every waking moment. And that...was to be with Eddie.

Eddie had a similar agenda, but with a few quirks added. Eddie was the kind of guy who had other things to concentrate on besides school. One of the few words he knew how to spell was trouble. Eddie's favorite possession and what he brazenly called his weapon of choice, was his Swiss Army knife. The joke around school was that all of its blades were sharper than he was. Eddie mistakenly flashed it one day when he got into a fight with one of the school toughs and promptly found himself liberated from it.

When the conversation turned to Eddie, Casey, as usual, did her best to avoid the subject. As she closed her locker, she gave it one last pat good-bye. Laden down with her old notebooks and used school supplies, she quickly off-loaded some onto Mandy and asked, "Where's your stuff?"

"Tossed it," Mandy replied.

As the two girls walked down the hall towards the front door to freedom, Mandy looked over at Casey excitedly, "You comin' up to the creek this week-end? Should be a lot of cute guys there. We could have a real good time."

Casey shrugged. "Can't. Lilly's home for the summer. Mom's working. So, I gotta stay with her."

Mandy did not attempt to hide her displeasure. "Oh, please. It's the same thing every summer. All you do is look after your little sister. It is real-ly gettin' to be a hassle!"

Casey had heard her friend's argument before. She didn't bother to respond as the girls exited the front doors of the school.

As they walked outside into the warmth of a beautiful Spring day, Casey's face practically lit up. She grabbed Mandy's arm, bringing her friend to a sudden halt.

"What?!" insisted a startled Mandy.

"Sh-s-ss. Listen!" Casey commanded.

They both stood perfectly still. Then suddenly, they heard it. The sound of the school's front doors closing shut. Casey sighed to herself and then looked at her friend, "Is that the best sound you've ever heard...or what?!"

43

Mandy practically squealed. "Yeah," she said, delighted, "nothing I like better than kissing this joint off for three months." Mandy began to turn around to give a big raspberry to the school. Casey quickly grabbed her arm.

"Uh-uh, don't look back. It spoils it."

Mandy laughed, keeping her eyes directed forward.

As they were heading down the steps, Mandy glanced off to the left. A saucy smile crossed her face as she stopped in her tracks. Casey stopped a half foot in front of her, looked back at her and then glanced in the direction Mandy was looking.

About a half block away, out by the curb, the two girls could see Eddie Burkette, Mandy's boyfriend. He was leaning over a revved up 1963 black Pontiac Catalina. Neither of the girls paid much attention to the car since they were unable to make out who Eddie was talking to and were clearly out of earshot of what was being said. Casey sighed. She would rather avoid Eddie all together, but Mandy's focus was on her man.

Eddie Burkette was a tall, lanky eighteen-year-old with a wayward shock of brown hair. He had a slight build that left him too lean to play sports. And, though he was the last to know it, he was far from being handsome enough to do much damage with the girls. Never among the swiftest kids on the school yard, he had been left back a grade for his less than stellar performance in Junior High School. High School turned out to be equally dismal. For Eddie, it was an academic obstacle course. One he would rather not run. But, none of that mattered to Mandy. She seemed to see something in him that no one else could.

Enamored, Mandy stared at Eddie and gloated, "Tell me that isn't one good-lookin' hunk-of-man."

Casey again found herself at a loss for words. No comment being the best comment, she smiled meekly -- neither agreeing nor disagreeing.

Eddie had both of his hands propped against the side of the Pontiac and was leaning in towards the passenger side window talking to one of its occupants. Suddenly, an arm reached out of the window of the Pontiac, grabbed Eddie by the shirt and yanked him flat up against the car. Eddie became animated, swinging his arms and gesturing as if trying to reassure someone. Casey looked at Mandy, concerned.

"What's going on?" she asked.

Mandy just laughed. "You know Eddie. He's just clowning around."

"Who are those guys?"

Mandy smirked and gave her a dubious look. "Oh yeah, right. Like I can keep up with the jokers Eddie screws around with. It's like he's always got something going on. I stopped keepin' track a long time ago."

The girls vantage point from the steps left them clueless regarding Eddie's true predicament.

From Eddie's close-up and far more personal perspective, however, the circumstances had definitely turned serious. In an effort to further emphasize to Eddie the overall gravity of his situation, Eddie was once again yanked forward by his assailant. His head and upper body disappeared inside the passenger window providing him a clearer, but unwanted, view of the three tough looking guys inside.

An older guy in a black, cut-off tee-shirt, with a line of tattoos down his arm, gripped Eddie's shirt tightly in his fist. He yanked Eddie closer. Alarmed, Eddie could feel the guy's hot breath as an angry sneer crossed the man's face.

"You got any idea what happens to people who mess with me?"

Eddie scrambled for an answer, "Mole, it was a foul-up. It wasn't my fault."

"Not buyin' it, Burkette. You either bring me the stuff or get me the money."

Mole again tightened his grip on Eddie's shirt, "Hear what I'm sayin', cowboy?"

It had been a few years since Mole had set foot in a high school -- and even then, it wasn't in the pursuit of a higher education. Mole was one of those guys who seemed to come from the wrong side of everywhere. His jet black hair and cold-as-steel eyes gave him the look of a predator. Even on his good days there was something dangerous about him. But, that day with Eddie he was downright sinister.

He pulled Eddie within an inch of his pock-marked face and snarled, "I asked you a question. Do you hear me?"

"Yeah...yeah, Mole, I hear ya."

Mole quickly released his grip sending Eddie sprawling to the ground. Pointing a menacing finger at him, Mole gave Eddie a look that would shatter granite.

"Don't...screw with me, little man. That is one mistake you don't wanna make."

He motioned to the driver, a weasel-looking guy, who upon Mole's command gunned the car's engine loudly. Eddie watched, speechless, as the three of them sped off, recklessly, away from the school.

Still shaken, Eddie got up, straightened his wrinkled shirt and looked around. He saw Mandy and Casey standing on the front steps of the school staring at him, stunned. Quickly regaining his composure, he waved and smiled. Then, flipping his collar up on the back of his neck and with whatever cool he had left, he strutted over to them as if nothing had happened. He met the girls at the bottom of the steps, grabbed Mandy around the waist and gave her a kiss.

Mandy quickly pulled away and demanded, "Eddie? What the hell was that?"

Eddie blew her off, "No big thing. Just foolin' around."

"Who were those guys?"

"Buds of mine from Rollyville. They're here doin' a little business."

"What kind of business?" she demanded.

"Hey. I said, it was nothin'."

"Nothin'! Then how come you just ended up with your butt on the ground?"

"I told you we were just horsin' around."

"Well, I don't like it."

"Hey! I bet the dude he couldn't hang on. I took a fall, but he lost." Eddie took a five dollar bill out of his pocket, showing it as proof. "It was just guy stuff. So, like I said, don't get your bun in a whirl, okay? Do I look upset?" he asked, flashing her one of his most winning smiles.

Succumbing to his charms, Mandy shook her head. "Uh-uh," she said as she coyly looped her finger through his belt. She pulled him close to her and then said seductively, "What you look is good enough to eat."

Eddie grinned and casually preened his hair, smoothing it down with the sweep of one hand, trying to look cool. "Well, Baby, feast your eyes all you want, 'cause what you see is what you're gonna get."

Mandy squealed with anticipation as he pranced around in a small circle in front of them. He was back in the saddle. As Eddie turned his attention to her, Casey let out a small groan. Stepping back to get a better look, he gave her the once over.

"Casey, you are lookin' fine today...how you doin'?"

Put off by his arrogance, Casey barely looked at him, "I'm okay."

Eddie gave her a Cheshire cat grin. "Well, that's just peachy." Once again feeling cocky, Eddie playfully grabbed at her and tugged on her violet blouse. As Casey smacked his hand away, Mandy giggled.

Eddie grinned at Casey and winked. "Hey, baby," he chided her, "you can't tell me you don't like it."

Casey looked at him like he was an idiot. But, Eddie was not discouraged.

Doing his best to show off in front of Casey, he whirled Mandy around and gave her a big, sensuous kiss full on the mouth.

Casey was unimpressed.

6) INDISCRETIONS & OPPOSITE ATTRACTIONS

Summers in Cedar Grove had a certain consistency. Always too short and never much different from the one before. It wasn't a cycle that was likely to be broken anytime soon. People in Cedar Grove didn't have a lot of money to spare on big out of town trips, so mostly what they did was just stay put. Not that it mattered to Casey. For her, it was the time of the year that always set things right. It was the time that brought her family back together.

The Castle house was once again a home -- as evidenced by the arrival of a pretty, young girl who was sitting at the small kitchen table, happily gulping down a glass of Coke. Lilly was finally home for the summer.

Though she had just turned eleven, her innocence -- and a general lack of preoccupation with things of the world -- made her look considerably younger. She sat at the table savoring her cold drink. Her mom was in the kitchen drying a few remaining dishes and stacking them neatly on the shelf. Camille was dressed in her olive and beige waitress' uniform, ready to go to work.

As the front door opened, Lilly looked up. She beamed when she saw her older sister. Casey immediately dumped her school supplies onto a an old rocking chair near the door and went over and gave Lilly a kiss.

"Hi, sweetie."

Casey called out to her mom in the kitchen, "Hi, Mom."

"Hi, doll," Camille answered.

Lilly held her glass out towards Casey and jiggled the ice.

"What," asked Casey, "you want some more?"

Lilly put the glass to her mouth, turned it upside down and tried to slurp down any remaining Coca Cola.

"Mom, I think she wants some more Coke."

Camille called out from the kitchen, "Uh-uh. No more Coke. She's ready to float away as is. Take her to the bathroom for me, will you?"

Casey shrugged at Lilly and took the glass away from her. As she tried to pull her up from the table, Lilly resisted. Casey pulled on her again. Refusing to budge, Lilly clung to her chair.

"She doesn't wanna."

Camille popped her head out of the kitchen, "I swear, Lilly, you're like a little camel."

Camille picked up her purse from one of the chairs. "Okay, young ladies, I'm out of here. Casey, here's a dollar for some tuna and chips." She handed her the money. "Now, I don't mind you watching TV, but don't let her stay up too late. And, sweetheart, would you mind folding the rest of the clothes. I didn't have time."

Casey put on a pout, "Mom, do you have to go to work tonight?"

"Yes, honey. One of the girls got sick. Besides, we need the money."

Camille kissed both her girls good-bye and was out the door.

Casey pocketed the money her mother gave her and looked around. She spotted Lilly's shoes and socks in front of the sofa. She went over and got them and took them over to where Lilly was seated.

"It's you and me, kiddo," she said as she pulled the socks over Lilly's feet. "What do you say...you wanna go get some tuna and chips?"

Lilly held her feet out for Casey to slip on the shoes. Lilly loved to "go" places. She smiled a sweet, gleeful smile and enthusiastically hopped out of the chair for their walk to the store. Casey smiled back at her and took her by the hand.

"Okay, then...let's go."

***

The main store in town was the Henke-Pillot. It was one of those big, new chain stores that seem to be popping up

50

everywhere. It had been said the Henke-Pillot had just about everything a body needs to eat. At least, that was the claim in the advertisement in the local paper. Everyone figured it wouldn't say it if it wasn't so.

With Lilly in hand and a dollar in her pocket, Casey headed inside the big store. Lilly was clearly enjoying her outing. She looked around at the tall shelves and stared up at the big fluorescent lights like she had just entered wonderland. As the two girls headed down one of the aisles, Casey was focused with a singular mission in mind. She was intently scanning the shelves for the canned tuna display. Finally, she spotted it. Just as she reached for a can, she was distracted by two women coming down the other side of the aisle. As the two women got closer, Casey felt her heart sink.

She could clearly see that they were whispering and gawking -- at Lilly. To make matters worse, they further compounded their rudeness by acting as if Casey wasn't even there. Casey recognized one of the women. It was the one and only Mrs. Eleanor Hotchkiss Creighton -- Cedar Grove's preeminent society matron.

Without warning, in mid-whisper, Mrs. Creighton abruptly shifted her attention from Lilly and planted her gaze directly on Casey. Her heavily lip-sticked mouth suddenly stretched like a large rubber band into a crimson half-moon as she gave Casey a condescending smile.

Her emotions in turmoil, Casey's mind raced. She most certainly had a thing or two she wanted to say to the both of them. But, as she found herself staring up into the face of one of Cedar Grove's most affluent and influential ladies, she was suddenly dumbstruck. Words escaped conscious thought as conflicting emotions overpowered her, leaving her speechless. By the time Casey regained her composure, the two women had scurried down the aisle, whispering and shaking their heads as they turned the corner.

Feeling awkward and oddly unsettled by the encounter, Casey did her best to shrug it off. Trying to ignore the feelings that it stirred inside, she turned her attention back to the tuna.

She lifted a can off of the shelf and then guided Lilly over to the aisle with the chips. Still feeling peculiarly disheartened, her thoughts were clearly not on the task at hand.

But, Lilly had no such distractions. For her, the rows of neatly stacked bags of potato chips were irresistible. As soon as she was within striking distance, Lilly reached out and made a grab for one of the large bags. Casey quickly yanked her hand back just in time with an emphatic, "No, Lilly!"

A young grocery stocker who was stacking a cookie display nearby, looked up and noticed the two girls. He and Casey glanced at each other. Casey casually reached for a smaller bag of chips, then eyed the cookie display.

"Tell you what," she said to Lilly, "if you're real good, we'll have some cookies for dessert."

It was fine with Lilly, she was just happy to be out and about. Without further delay, the girls headed straight for the cookie display. As Casey reached for a bag of cookies off of the top, Lilly made a fast grab for two bags in the middle. The young male stocker could not believe his eyes. Suddenly, there were cookies everywhere. Like a small avalanche, the display tumbled down on to the floor, scattering its wayward bundles around the girls' feet. The young male stocker was stunned.

"What the hell is she doin'!" he exclaimed loudly.

Casey looked at Lilly, aghast, "Lilly?!"

As luck would have it, Mrs. Creighton and her friend had managed to round the corner just in time to see the fiasco. Flustered, Casey looked up at Mrs. Creighton and then back at the angry stocker.

"I'm sorry. She didn't mean to..."

He interrupted her. "Everybody knows you don't take 'em from the middle, you take 'em from the top. What is she, *stupid* or something!"

"Hey!! Back off," she snapped, "I said I was sorry about your stupid cookies!"

Once more, shaking their heads and whispering, Mrs. Creighton and the other woman disappeared around the corner.

The young guy kneeled down and started gathering up the bags of cookies. Some had cascaded down and remained stacked one on top of the another.

Others had scattered pell mell across the grocery store's floor.

Displeased, he was still grumbling, "You have any idea how long this took me..."

"Look, I said, we were sorry...okay?" offered up Casey.

"Well, you can forget that...'cause sorry doesn't cut it," he groused at her.

"Fine with me," Casey retorted, "'cause I'm not saying it again!"

With that she reached down, picked up a large bag of cookies, grabbed Lilly's hand and headed for the check-out stand. Casey placed her tuna, chips and cookies down in front of the cashier.

Standing at the counter behind the two girls, checking out their purchases, were Mrs. Creighton and her friend. They watched Casey waiting to pay for her groceries. As if her day couldn't get any worse, Casey again heard Mrs. Creighton snickering and whispering -- this time just loud enough to be overheard.

"Pity, isn't it," she droned, "a young girl like that having to deal with such a *unbearable burden* all of her life." Mrs. Creighton's voice positively dripped with false sincerity.

In her most pitying tone, the other woman whispered back, "My, yes, what a shame for someone her age to be shackled with such an unfortunate problem."

As the women's words cut into the vulnerable, soft tissue of her young heart, Casey pretended not to hear. She did her best to ignore them as she slowly looked over at Lilly -- who, was now, on her best behavior and was innocently gazing about the big, shiny store. As Casey looked at her little sister, she felt a slight catch in her throat. She fought hard to stifle an onslaught of emotions as she choked back her tears.

Suddenly, she was interrupted by the cashier. "That'll be one-twenty-five."

"Wh...what?" said Casey, shaken from her stupor.

"That'll be one dollar and twenty-five cents," repeated the cashier.

Casey looked at the dollar in her hand, "I...I don't have enough."

The cashier looked at her and shrugged. Embarrassed, Casey looked down into her grocery bag. Disheartened, she grabbed the cookies and shoved them across the counter at him.

"Here...keep them," she insisted, "we didn't want them anyway."

Not able to bear another moment in that store, she tossed the dollar down as payment for the groceries, picked up the bag with the tuna and chips and grabbed Lilly's hand. As she hurried out of the store, the cashier looked up perplexed and called after her, "Hey...what about your change?"

***

As Casey and Lilly walked home from the store, the events at the Henke-Pillot continued to swirl around in her head. Though they were only a block from the house, there was not yet distance enough between the store and Casey to allow her to cool down. Still upset, she angrily aired her opinions to an attentive Lilly. "What do they know, anyway!? Mama says they're just ignorant people. They don't know anything about anything." She looked at Lilly with great consternation, "You ask me, they're the ones with the problem!"

Lilly looked at her big sister with an unblemished innocence and smiled. It was the kind of smile that always made Casey's heart melt just a little.

It was the kind of smile that made everything else seem unimportant. As she looked at Lilly's sweet, little face, it *broke* her anger. She smiled back and said with a renewed conviction, "We don't care, do we? They don't bother us!"

None of it mattered to Lilly. She was completely unaffected by the incidents at the store. As long as she was out for a walk with her big sister, everything was right with the world. Casey looked at her little sister and smiled, "I love you...you know that?"

As the two girls approached their house, a car passed by. The car abruptly pulled into Mrs. Eberworth's driveway next door. A young guy got out.

To Casey's amazement, it was the grocery stocker from the store. He stared at them both for a moment and then took out a key and went inside Mrs. Eberworth's house. Casey raised her eyebrows and looked at Lilly.

"Well now...doesn't that beat all."

***

Once inside their house, it didn't take Casey long to whip up some tuna sandwiches. It took her and Lilly even less time to eat them. Tuna fish sandwiches were standard Friday night fare and the girls never seemed to get tired of eating them along with their potato chips and Coke.

Once Casey had the dishes washed and put away, the girls were finally able to settle in. An old Motorola television blared out a commercial as Casey sat on the sofa folding towels and wash cloths. Perched beside her, already in her pajamas, was Lilly.

Casey had made sure that Lilly had her own towel to fold. Lilly was totally preoccupied with the towel, unfolding and refolding it, doing her best to mimic her big sister. Their's was a small family and everybody had to carry her load. Lilly was intent on doing her part.

When the TV commercials finally went off and the movie came back on, the announcer's voice blared out -- "We now return to our feature, 'Tarzan,' starring Johnny Weissmuller." Casey looked up at the TV.

"It's about time," she commented out loud.

Lilly, too, had become bored. She put down her towel and reached for another one in the middle of the neatly piled stack that Casey had already folded. Casey quickly stopped her, pulling her hand away.

"Easy, young lady," she said, giving Lilly a fresh towel to fold. "Here's a nice yellow one. Work on that for a while."

Lilly was not particular. The faded yellow towel would do just fine.

As Lilly began folding her towel, there was a knock at the door. Surprised, Casey looked at Lilly. "You expecting somebody?" she asked.

Lilly gave her a blank stare.

Casey put her towels down on the sofa and went to the door and opened it. She gasped as she quickly covered her mouth with her hand. Standing there, with a bruise on her face and a swollen eye, was Mandy. Casey was shocked at the sight of her friend.

"Mandy! Oh, my God, what happened to you?"

Unable to speak, Mandy stared up at Casey. Her bruised and swollen face suddenly became contorted as it scrunched up into a tight little knot and she started to cry. Casey looked around quickly and then brought her friend inside.

"Did Eddie do this to you?"

Mandy wasn't able to stop her crying long enough to give a coherent answer. Unsettled at the sight of her friend, Casey anxiously looked over at Lilly and then said to Mandy, "Don't move, okay. I've gotta put Lilly to bed. Just...stay put. I'll be right back."

When Casey took Lilly by the hand and led her out of the room, Mandy collapsed onto the sofa. She sobbed loudly and buried her head into the stack of freshly folded towels.

Casey returned quickly. Seeing her friend face down in the fresh laundry, she went to her side to comfort her.

"My God, Mandy, tell me what happened."

Red-eyed, Mandy looked up at Casey. She wiped her eyes with one of the towels and attempted to explain.

"After school, Eddie told me that his dad 'bummed out' on him and that he's not going to California after all. That's great news. I mean, you know...I was really excited. So, we went to my house to celebrate." Mandy struggled to hold back her sobs.

"We were having a really good time...then, my dad came home early from work and he...he caught us."

"Caught you?"

"Yeah. I was modeling my yellow bikini for Eddie and...well, one thing led to the other...and, we sort of *did it*," she sobbed.

"You sort of *did it*?"

"It was terrible. My dad threw Eddie out... "

Casey was still confused, "How do you *'sort of'* do it?" Mandy was not listening. "When my dad came back into my room, he said he could never hold his head up high again in this town. Oh, please," she said incredulously, "he's just a dufus used car salesman. How the hell 'high' could he hold it up anyway?"

Casey looked at her, stunned. "I don't think that's the point, Mandy."

"When I told him he couldn't stop me from seeing Eddie, he got really mad. He started beating on me. My mom finally got home from work and..." she broke down again, "...and made him stop."

Horrified by Mandy's ordeal, Casey hugged her friend, doing her best to console her. She then looked at her in utter amazement, "I can't believe you actually...did it."

Mandy hesitated. "Yeah, well...it's not exactly like it's the first time."

Casey looked at her, shocked at the confession.

"Wait a minute. What are you saying?"

"I'm sayin'...it's not like it's the first time."

"You mean...with Eddie?"

"Of course, with Eddie."

Casey was stunned, having just been hit with a double whammy.

Before she could respond, Lilly suddenly reappeared in the hallway. As badly as she wanted to pursue the conversation, Casey had to attend to her younger sister, "Uh, Mandy, uh...Lilly has to go to the bathroom. Look, I've got to help her, okay?"

"Help her?!"

"Yeah...whatever. Okay?" Casey offered no further explanation.

Mandy shrugged, "Okay. Do what you gotta do. I've got to get home anyway before my dad finds out I'm gone."

Casey looked at her pal. Troubled by what she had just heard, she fidgeted a bit, knowing full well she had to say something. She knew Mandy might not like it...still, she needed to say it. Casey took a deep breath and spoke her mind.

"Mandy...look," she said hesitantly, "you know, maybe your dad had his reasons for being upset. I mean, if you think about it..."

Casey suddenly stopped cold. Mandy's face was just short of volcanic. She glared at Casey in a rage. It was as if a red flare had gone off behind Mandy's eyes.

Shocked by her friend's sudden anger, Casey tried to explain, "Look, all I'm trying to say is..."

"Oh please, spare me," Mandy angrily interrupted. "I can't believe what I'm hearing," she yelled indignantly. "Give me a freakin' break!" Mandy's voice was practically spewing her scorn. "I can't believe you're taking his side!"

"Mandy...wait a minute. I'm just saying you have to consider, it had to be a shock to find his own daughter...in his own house. I mean, after all, he's your dad."

Angered even more by her defense, Mandy jumped up from the sofa. Her voice filled with vitriol, she screamed down at Casey, "What the hell do you know about it, anyway?! <u>You don't even have a dad!</u>"

Stunned by Mandy's outburst, Casey was caught completely off guard. She again tried to explain, "Mandy, will you listen a minute? I was just trying to say, that he may have had a reason to be upset -- but, he never, never should have hit you."

"Damn right, he shouldn't. I just hope he took his best shots," Mandy said more to herself than to Casey, "'cause he's never gonna do it again." As she stood there in the middle of the small living room, Mandy's mind began flashing its own private and graphic vision of revenge against her father. She was far too

58

immersed in her own imaginings to notice that Casey's thoughts had also drifted elsewhere.

The room was suddenly quiet and still. An uncustomary, lingering silence seemed to separate the two girls like an unseen line of demarcation.

Feelings of betrayal suddenly propelled Mandy from her innermost thoughts back to the reality of the moment. She realized the betrayal was not hers, but Casey's. She looked over at a very despondent Casey who was still off in her own world as she sat quietly among the disheveled towels and wash cloths.

Sensing her friend's anguish and feeling a tinge of guilt, Mandy finally began to calm down. Somewhat timidly, she went over to Casey.

"Case?" she said, softly.

Casey responded sharply, "What?"

Mandy winced slightly. She knew she deserved it. She was the one who overreacted and she knew she was the one who needed to make amends. "Look, I'm...I'm really sorry," Mandy said sincerely, "about that crack about your dad. I didn't mean anything by it."

Casey looked at her for a moment and then shrugged, "Don't worry about it. What is...is. I've just gotta learn to 'get over it and get on with it,' you know?"

"Yeah, well, sometimes I can be a real dodo brain."

Casey looked at her, "What? You expecting me to disagree with you?"

Mandy chuckled and then leaned over and gave Casey a hug. "Buds?" she asked hopefully.

"Buds," Casey replied smiling and hugging her back.

No sooner was the matter resolved, than Mandy was back on her feet and on the move again.

"I gotta go," she said, "before the wardens come by and start checking my cell."

Casey stared at her friend in disbelief, "I can't believe you snuck out. I mean...along with everything else."

An impish grin spread across Mandy's bruised face as she headed for the door, "Hey...a girl's gotta do what a girl's gotta do...and nobody's gonna stop this girl from doin' it!"

With that, Mandy blew her a kiss good-bye, turned on her heel and disappeared out of the door.

7) UNEXPECTED ENCOUNTERS

On a typical, warm Friday night in June, it wasn't likely a person could find much stirring in Cedar Grove, except for the crickets and lightning bugs and an occasional stray dog. It was like somebody flipped off the switch and no one had the inclination or energy to flip it back on. Just like all of the other evenings during the week, Fridays lazily rolled by one after the other with nothing special to do and no particular place to go.

But, every summer, there was at least one very special Friday night that was a whole sight different from the rest. Some folks tended to frown on it, but others found themselves highly titillated with sheer anticipation. The whole town knew that if a person was looking for a little excitement, all they had to do was drive a mere twenty miles outside the city limits of Cedar Grove across the county line. The big night had finally arrived and there had been talk since early May that this year things were really going to be shaking.

An Adults Only affair, it portended to be a hot night on the town for anyone willing to venture beyond the environs of Cedar Grove. And, it was evident from the looks of the crowded two lane highway leading out of town that the exodus had begun.

There was a touch of electricity in the air as cars of all descriptions streamed off the highway onto a large, dirt parking lot about the size of a football field. Cadillacs and farm trucks alike vied for every available spot. The bright neon lights of the Delta Blues Nightclub illuminated the darkness as an air of excitement surrounded the black owned nightclub. It was a night that white and black patrons alike were looking forward to as they swarmed from a tri-county area into the club. Everyone was anxious to move to the rhythm and blues sounds of Bobby T. James and the JamesBoys.

Bobby T. was long revered in the same circles as Bobby Blue Bland and B.B. King, making the night an event not to be missed.

Inside the club, smartly dressed patrons, wearing everything from sequins and lace to polyester and tissue lamé, anxiously crowded up front to tables that had been shoved close together on the club's main dance floor. Many had arrived an hour early in order to be near the bandstand. Several overly zealous fashion mavens blatantly ignored the summer heat and draped themselves in their finest fox furs for the momentous occasion. The Delta Blues was, after all, the place to see and be seen. Considering, of course, the purpose for being there...was the entertainment. But then, not all of its patrons were attracted to the Delta Blues for the right reasons.

Regardless, anticipation was high, as folks came from far and wide for the summer's big show. As the club began to fill to capacity, a local band did its best to entertain the eager, multiethnic crowd.

King Luther, the club's effusive owner, appeared to be in perpetual motion in the middle of the organized mayhem, doing what he always did best, meeting, greeting and working the room. With the King around, nobody who entered escaped a firm pat on the back or a hearty handshake.

Luther was a very large, black man who moved with the agility of a gazelle. As he glided through the crowd, he cracked orders to his staff to render service at a faster pace to his burgeoning room of customers. Unceasingly effervescent, he had a smile brighter than a sunrise, which he was never too shy to admit, had been handsomely paid for. He was known to flash his pearly white porcelains at the slightest inducement and then proceed to describe in great detail how they miraculously managed to conceal years of childhood neglect.

Luther enthusiastically extended a greeting to a party of four when he spotted a sharp looking couple, making their way through the crowd towards the bandstand. Catching their eye, he waved as he went over to meet his old friends. Reaching out his big, beefy hands, he grabbed the man by the shoulders, pulled him close and gave him a friendly bear hug.

"Calvin, how you doing, man? It is an honor to have you in my club."

Feigning indifference, Calvin pretended to be unaffected by Luther's gracious reception, "Well, the Waffle House was closed for the evening. So LuAnn and I figured this being the next best thing, we'd go ahead and stop on by."

Rolling her eyes skyward, LuAnn looked at Calvin and snickered, "Like Luther's gonna believe a word you're saying. Luther, don't pay any attention to him. Coming here is all he's talked about for weeks now."

Luther laughed, then smiled at LuAnn. From the first time he had met her, he had always had a thing for her, but was far too much of a gentleman to ever let it show. She was Calvin's woman. And Calvin was a friend.

Still, he couldn't help notice how stunning she looked in her simple, black sheath dress held up by the thinnest of spaghetti straps. He could see that she had taken great pains with her hair as it laid across her head in perfectly spaced finger waves. He felt his pulse race as the lights from the bar illuminated the sheen that seemed to glow off of her ebony shoulders. Then, as if compelled to interrupt his own thoughts, Luther reached out and gently took her hand in his.

"LuAnn, you are by far the finest looking thing that has walked through that door this evening."

Calvin pretended to take offense. "And just what am I..." he demanded as he executed a perfect spin, showing off his glimmering, new aqua-blue, acetate-satin suit to Luther, "some old junk yard dog?"

Luther stepped back to get a good look at him "My heavens!! Would you look at you." Luther couldn't resist goading his good friend. "Lord, Calvin, I will never understand how you ever got next to a woman like this."

Calvin was quick to retaliate. "It's 'cause the woman has got taste. Something you obviously know nothin' about."

"Taste, uh? Well, if she ever gets a bite of a grade-A top sirloin, I guarantee she ain't never going back to some funky-old butt-end ground round. Isn't that right, Sugar?"

LuAnn pretended to referee, "Now, you boys behave." She looked at Luther, coyly. "Luther, honey, I'm not saying sirloin's not a special treat, but a girl can make ground round go a whole lot further...if she knows what to do with it."

Luther smiled warmly at LuAnn. Then giving her his most sympathetic look, he nodded his head in agreement.

"You're right. I suppose a lady's gotta do the best with what she's got."

Calvin was geared up to deliver his final zing, but found himself sidetracked as a member of Luther's staff slid up next to Luther and started whispering in his boss' ear.

Luther paused for a brief moment to hear what the man had to say. It was obvious the man was rankled about something. He glowered across the crowded room towards the bar. "That white dude...Weasel, is here," the man said with disdain.

King Luther followed the man's line of sight and looked over at the bar.

Sitting there alone was a smallish, white guy who looked like he was doing a bad James Dean impression. It was the weasel-looking driver of the black Pontiac that was at the high school earlier. He had been with the guy with the arm full of tattoos who had given Eddie Burkette a hard time.

Seeing that he had attracted King Luther's attention, Weasel looked back at him. Emboldened, he raised his glass and nodded brazenly as if he were one of King Luther's invited guest. Luther was not pleased. But, now was not the time to deal with the little pest. The time had come for him to introduce Bobby T. and his band.

Luther turned his attention back to Calvin and LuAnn.

"Ya'll better find your seats. I got a table with your name on it up front. Anything you want, you let one of my people know, okay?"

"Thanks, man. When you take a break, come on over and join us," offered Calvin as the couple quickly took his advice

64

and hurriedly made their way to their table to enjoy the evening's show.

Luther waved a high sign to the drummer for the house band to begin playing his intro. As the drum roll began, the room fell silent. There was a buzz of anticipation as Luther cut a swath through the crowd. Then, with an explosive burst of energy, he bounded up the steps and onto the stage. In perfect rhythm with the band, he performed some fancy foot work before grabbing the microphone off of its stand. As he stood in the glow of the spot lights, his larger than life persona permeated the nightclub.

With a great bluster, King Luther began to rev up his audience.

Swinging the mike around him with the panache of a showman, he let it circle through the air a couple of times, then grabbed it mid-rotation with one hand as the drummer clanged his cymbals. With the sound reverberating throughout the room, Luther smiled one of his broadest and most charismatic smiles. The audience began to cheer.

Gazing out over the crowd, he could see the place was packed. He knew full well what they had come for and he was ready to give it to them.

"Are we ready to move our souls...right down to our very toes!!" he yelled enthusiastically into the microphone. The audience screamed its approval and applauded with wild expectation. As they did so, the warm-up band seemingly faded away, disappearing behind the curtains. Within seconds, the JamesBoys were on stage behind Luther, setting up their instruments. The drummer gave a drum roll that was met with more cheers and screaming.

King Luther beamed at the crowd and bellowed out, "Who is the King?"

He joyously cupped his hand to his ear as the crowd repeatedly yelled, "LUTHER...LUTHER....LUTHER." It was a love fest.

"That's right. That's me, KING LUTHER. And since I am your King...and I rule this roost...I order every last one of my loyal subjects -- to leave your worries at the door...get your shoes on the floor and rock this house...till it can't take it no more!"

Whoops and cheers from the crowd electrified the room. King Luther was now ready to give them what they wanted and he did so with a great flourish.

"It is now with great pleasure that the Delta Blues Nightclub presents to you this evening, *a man* -- that's got that white boy from Memphis takin' notes... B.B. King tossin' in his sleep...and Little Richard screamin' out loud *when he ain't got no crowd*...the man who took the sound from the ground... put the blues in the Delta...and, tonight, money in my pocket! Brothers and sisters, put your hands together for one of the great rhythm and blues artists of our time... BOBBY T. JAMES AND THE JAMESBOYS!!"

Bobby T. whirled and gyrated onto the stage playing to the highly receptive crowd. His band immediately began rocking the house with a song that set the audience on fire. More than satisfied with the reaction, King Luther boogied his way off stage to the delight of onlookers.

As the music rocked the rafters, hardly anyone noticed a minor ruckus at the front door as two men got into a shoving match. As the bouncers settled the argument, Eddie Burkette strutted his way through the club's front entrance.

Eddie was slicked down, greased up and walked with a stride that said he was "too cool for the room." As he made his way through the crowd, he unwittingly caught the attention of Weasel. Unaware his presence had been noted, Eddie looked around and took up a position at the end of the bar that allowed him to survey the action. It was not long before he got what he came for. Weasel watched curiously as two black guys came over to Eddie, made an exchange of some kind and left.

As the band struck up another song, a white man and woman approached Eddie. The woman appeared anxious as she slipped some money into Eddie's hand. With the money secured, Eddie then reached over, glad-handed the man and palmed him a small packet. The packet, filled with a white powdery substance, slipped from the man's hand and fell to the floor. The man looked around nervously, then picked up the packet and pocketed it. Doing his best to appear nonchalant, Eddie bobbed his head back and forth to the rhythm of the music as the two quickly walked away. Eddie sat there feeling slicker than high-gloss Shinola on a fine pair of patent leathers. He was getting damn good, he thought to himself. Once again, everything went down as smooth as glass.

Unfortunately, neither of the transactions had gone unnoticed -- either by the beady-eyed Weasel or the wary bartender. Without changing expression, the bartender nodded to one of the bouncers. Before Eddie knew which end was up, he was lifted off his barstool by a couple of very husky men, hauled across the room and muscled out of the front door. It wasn't that unusual to see somebody getting thrown out of the Delta Blues. Nobody paid it much mind, since most figured trouble-making riff-raff was better off 'out the door' anyway.

***

Once outside, the two men dragged Eddie to the side of the building and tossed him down to the ground between two cars.

"Hey...hey...hey!" he yelled at them as he hit the dirt, "Whataya think you're doin'?"

As Eddie was about to get up, King Luther rounded a corner. There was none of the ebullience that he had shown on stage. His very size and demeanor alone posed a serious threat. Seeing him, Eddie tried to scramble to his feet. One of the bouncers shoved him back down in the dirt. As King Luther towered over him, Eddie's heart pounded. Luther glared down at him.

"You think you can come into my place and do your dirty business...in front of my customers...in front of my staff...and in front of ME!?" he boomed. "This ain't the first time I've seen you here dealin' that filth."

"I don't know what you're talkin' about," Eddie said, trying to maintain his innocence. "I swear I didn't do nothin'."

"I suggest you shut-up and listen," growled Luther, "'cause you are never gonna hear me say this again." He was in no mood to cut Eddie any slack.

"This is my club. You don't come in it anymore," he warned. "You're swimmin' in a dirty pond, boy. It is loaded with some very big and very bad sharks." King Luther got right in Eddie's face, "And, I'm not about to put up with some upstart white boy who's about to get his head bit off. You understand me?"

Eddie nervously looked at the three large men. He nodded his head rapidly. "Yeah...yeah, I got it, I understand."

With one swoop of his big, beefy hand, King Luther reached down and yanked Eddie up on his feet by his shirt collar. Eddie cringed as the two bouncers grabbed him by his arms, holding him steady. King Luther smirked, then reached into Eddie's front pocket and pulled out the money he had made on the dope deals. Eddie was mortified.

King Luther counted out half, snickered -- then threw the rest on the ground in front of Eddie. The two bouncers released their grip. One shoved him backwards, again knocking him off his feet. As they all turned and walked away, Eddie remained on the ground, not daring to make a move. He waited until he felt certain that the three men had gone back inside the nightclub, then taking his chances, he scrambled in the dirt, quickly scooping up the remaining money.

***

Weeks later and seemingly world's apart, it was a beautiful summer's day at Cedar Creek. Sounds of swimmers splashing in the cool creek waters could be heard as children played on the grass. The picnic grounds were filled with families who were out for a relaxing summer's day.

A short distance away, a section for sun bathers was crowded with teenagers. At the far end of the grounds, beyond the sun bathers -- an old, wooden bridge crossed over the creek, leading to a heavily wooded area.

Back where the families had gathered, Camille, Casey and Lilly had already staked out one of the picnic tables. Camille reached into a drink cooler and pulled out a Coke for Lilly. Lilly looked at the Coke excitedly.

Camille smiled and gave it to her, "Here you go, sweetie."

Somewhat dubious, Casey watched her little sister slurp down the soda,

"I think she's addicted to those things."

Camille smiled and looked at Casey, "You want one?"

"You bet," she said without hesitation.

They both laughed. It was a good day to be together.

***

Over in the sun bathers' section, Mandy was sprawled face down on a blanket in short shorts and a halter top listening to an old Janice Joplin song on a portable radio. Just as she was about to shift positions, Eddie plopped down next to her, rolled her over and started kissing her. She giggled, then eyed him suspiciously, "You're late."

"Ain't no big thing," he kissed her again. "'Cause I am here now."

"You better not be hanging with some other girl."

"What? You heard somethin'?" he teased.

"Wise acre," she retorted.

Eddie laughed and reached into her nearby drink cooler. He pulled out two beers. He was pleased. "Good girl. Hit your old man's supply again."

"Yeah...like he's ever gonna miss 'em."

They both leaned back and began drinking their beers. Eddie again looked at Mandy. He reached over, wrapped her hair around one of his fingers and aimlessly twisted it. She looked back at him and smiled.

"Is this the life, or what?"

Eddie didn't answer. He just looked at her. He stopped twirling her hair and propped himself up on one elbow. "I been

69

thinkin'," he pondered for a moment. "Whataya say we split this town?"

Mandy smiled. Relishing his display of affection, she took his hand and kissed it, "I'm with you, Baby...one more year and we're outta here. We'll ditch this dirt mound and never look back."

Eddie sat up straight. "No! You're not listenin'. I'm not talkin' a year. I'm talkin' now!"

Mandy was stunned, "Now?"

"Yeah," he continued. "I gotta get outta here," he said emphatically.

"This town is Losersville. It's crampin' my style."

Mandy rolled over, lying face up on her blanket. It was obvious, she was not taking him seriously.

"I swear, sometimes you say the craziest things."

"What the hell we gotta stay for?" he insisted, leaning over her again.

She looked up at him. "Eddie. We've got school. Besides, where will we go? You gotta have money to do something like that."

Eddie leaned down closer. He had a determined look in his eye. "I got a stash," he said emphatically. "You hear what I'm sayin'...a real stash. And, I'm not just talking traveling money."

She shoved him back, playfully, and teased, "Yeah, right. What'd you do, rob a bank?"

Suddenly, a large shadow blocked their sun. They both looked up to see a big guy standing over them. Next to him was the smaller guy, Weasel, from the nightclub.

Weasel tapped Eddie's leg with his foot. "Let's go," he ordered.

Eddie looked at them, somewhat annoyed, "Not now, guys."

Weasel was having none of it. "I said, let's go."

Eddie again tried to blow him off. "Hey, give me a break. I'm busy here, okay?"

The two characters looked at each other and smirked.

"Now, ain't that somethin'," said Weasel sarcastically. "You hear that, Loverboy here ain't got time for us...he's busy."

The big guy, called Bull, grunted as he looked over at Mandy, "I wouldn't mind stayin' busy myself. Maybe sweet-cheeks here would like to join us?"

Eddie jumped up, defensively.

Mandy looked up disgusted and then demanded of Eddie, "Who are these creeps?"

Bull eyed Mandy, "Hey, hey, now...be nice, we're just tryin' to be sociable."

Weasel snickered, "Yeah, relax, baby doll, don't make this into somethin' it ain't.

As Weasel and Bull focused their attention on Mandy, Eddie realized he had to act quickly. He carefully slid his hand down into the back pocket of his cut-off jeans and pulled out a small object. He then reached down, took Mandy by the hand and pulled her to her feet. As he did so, he slipped the object he had gotten out of his back pocket into her hand. Pulling her towards him, he gave her a quick kiss and whispered in her ear, "Don't tell nobody I gave you this."

Mandy looked at him anxiously, "Eddie, what's going on?"

"Nothin' I can't handle, Baby. Everything's cool. You just go on home now. Boys and me...we got some business to discuss."

He patted her on the cheek and left with Bull and Weasel. As Eddie walked off towards the bridge with the two older looking guys, Mandy looked down at the object in her hand. It was a *small key*. She watched curiously as the three crossed the bridge and disappeared into the wooded area. Confused about what had just happened and uncertain as to what to do about it, she sat back down on her blanket. She stared at the small key in her hand. She scrutinized it intently -- hoping somehow upon closer examination, it would unlock its purpose. Perplexed, she took another sip of her beer. Then doing as Eddie said -- she loaded the stray empty bottles into her cooler, picked up her radio, threw her blanket over her shoulder and left for home.

***

Back in the picnic area, the pleasant calm of the summer's day remained virtually uninterrupted. Camille was spreading a checkered table cloth that she had borrowed from the restaurant across the picnic table. As she was doing so, she looked over at Casey and Lilly. The two girls were sitting on the grass, watching the swimmers. One of the swimmers had caught Casey's eye. It was the young grocery stocker from the Henke-Pillot. She couldn't help but notice that there was something altogether different about him as his taut, tanned physique gleamed in the noon day sun.

"Mom," she called out, "see that guy out there?"

Her mother followed her gaze. "What about him?"

"I saw him go into Mrs. Eberworth's house the other day. He used a key."

Her mother took a better look, "Oh, that must be Mrs. Eberworth's grandson. He's here to help out until she gets over her operation."

Casey was intrigued, "Really?"

"Uh-huh," her mother continued, "I think his name is Chance."

"Chance? What kind of name is that?"

"Good as any, I suppose."

Camille then directed her attention towards Lilly. "Casey, why don't you take Lilly for a walk. I'm sure she can use the exercise."

Casey could not take her eyes off of Chance.

"Uh...what?" she mumbled.

"Your sister. Walk. Exercise."

"Yeah, good idea, Mom." This time, her mother's words made perfect sense. "You're absolutely right. Wouldn't hurt to get in a little sight-seeing before lunch."

Seizing the opportunity, Casey got up, took Lilly by the hand and the two started walking in the direction of the bridge. She glanced towards Chance as they passed by the water. He looked up and saw them. Casey pretended not to notice and kept walking. Chance continued to watch them as they headed towards the old bridge.

***

Across the bridge, on the opposite side of the creek, things were not so pleasant. The three tough looking guys who had hassled Eddie in front of school, now had him surrounded in the wooded area. Mole, their leader, was in the middle of his interrogation.

"I got no patience for this, cowboy. Your mouth keeps moving but you ain't tellin' me what I want to know."

Eddie was seriously panicked, "Mole, I told you, I went to pick up the stuff and it wasn't there."

"Now, that is what I call unfortunate, Burkette." Mole sneered at him, "'Cause things start gettin' real nasty, real fast when some joker interrupts the flow in the pipeline." Mole grabbed Eddie by the jaw. He squeezed, hard. Eddie was too scared to even flinch.

"Listen to me, punk, I got people to answer to. Right now they're givin' me serious heat. They're expectin' their stuff up north. And, here you are...some small town piece of crap makin' me look bad."

Feeling Mole's hot breath on his face, Eddie scrambled for an explanation.

"You gotta listen to me, Mole. I'm not the one doin' ya. It was the guy who was suppose to make the delivery. He didn't do the drop."

Mole loosened his grip. He patted Eddie's face. "You think so?"

"Oh yeah, he's the bum who stiffed ya, Mole. I'm sure of it."

"That's how you figure it?"

"Yeah...I'm tellin' ya, he's the one you gotta nail," Eddie assured him.

Mole looked at him coolly. "Could be you're on to something. Problem is, Burkette, my brother-in-law did the drop. So, you tell me, who am I supposed to believe...you or family?"

Hearing Mole's revelation, panic started to flood through Eddie's body like a tidal wave. His heart pounded and sweat poured down his face as the three men moved towards him.

***

Completely unaware of what was happening on the other side, Casey and Lilly crossed the bridge. They were heading straight towards the wooded area. Casey had turned their walk into a nature hike, having spotted a patch of yellow sunflowers.

"Look, Lilly...aren't they beautiful. We'll pick some and take them back to Mama, okay?"

Once they had crossed the bridge, Casey carefully guided Lilly over some underbrush to an old tree stump and lifted her onto it. Lilly gleefully looked around, enjoying her adventure.

"All right, stay put," Casey directed her, "I'll get the flowers."

Casey went over and began picking some of the large, yellow flowers. As she reached for a smaller one, a hand reached down and plucked it from her grasp. She looked up. It was Chance. As she got up, he graciously extended the flower towards her.

"I just want to say I'm sorry."

"About what?" she asked.

"About Lilly. About the way I acted. My grandmother told me that, you know, that she doesn't talk...and all. I guess I made a real idiot out of myself."

"Well, I wouldn't go that far," said Casey.

He looked over at Lilly. "It's just that she looks so...so normal."

Casey nodded, understanding, "She does, doesn't she?"

"I just wanted you to know that I really didn't mean anything by it," he said, apologetically.

As they looked at each other for a moment, Chance once more extended his arm, offering her the sunflower.

As she took it, he smiled shyly. Casey blushed.

With Casey and Chance momentarily fixated on one another, Lilly had managed to slip down, unnoticed, off the tree stump and was walking deeper into the wooded area. Attracted by the sounds she was hearing, she came to a clearing in the trees, then stopped for a moment and stared.

In clear sight, she saw the three toughs hassling Eddie. She watched as Weasel and Bull held Eddie against a tree. Mole stepped up to him, grabbed him by his hair and hit him hard in the solar plexus. Eddie doubled over in pain. His face was badly swollen. Blood trickled from his mouth.

Mole hit him again and sneered, "What you are...punk, is an example. You're like a message to the rest of the yokels, not to screw with me...or the organization."

Mole hit Eddie again, hard, causing Eddie to spit up more blood.

"What were you planning, huh? You think you were gonna set up shop and sell it right out from under me?"

Infuriated, Mole cracked Eddie across the jaw. Eddie's head slammed hard backwards into the tree, his body went limp, he slumped to the ground.

Mole and the others looked down at him. Mole nudged Eddie's body with his foot. There was no response.

Mole looked at the lifeless body with disgust. Without a hint of remorse, he issued the order, "Dump him."

As the other two started to move Eddie's body, Mole cautiously looked around, making certain their actions had gone undetected. Suddenly, his eyes hardened and narrowed into slits. He saw Lilly looking straight at him. He growled menacingly under his breath to the others, "We got trouble."

Bull and Weasel stopped what they were doing. Bull asked, "What..." as the two men followed Mole's gaze. They looked directly at Lilly. Lilly made no attempt to get away. She just stood there, calmly staring back. Mole growled to his two henchmen, "Get her!"

Before the two could make their move towards Lilly, they suddenly heard a male voice calling out.

"Lilly! Lilly!"

Mole, Bull and Weasel quickly ducked behind some bushes. Panicked, Bull looked over at Mole, "Whatta we gonna do, Mole?"

Mole glared at him, "Shut up."

Hearing her name, Lilly had already turned around. Relieved to see her, Chance started walking towards her.

"There you are." He smiled at her. "You really had us worried there for a minute. Casey! I found her!"

Casey hurriedly made her way through the thicket. She was obviously very shaken. Mole watched from the bushes as Casey approached the others.

He could see that she was upset, but very relieved to see the young girl.

"Oh, thank God!" She grabbed Lilly and hugged her, "Lilly, you scared me to death. What am I gonna to do with you?" Sensing her concern, Lilly gave her sister a puzzled look and smiled.

Chance tried to calm Casey by making light of the situation, "She was just out having an adventure...weren't you, Lilly?"

Casey eyed Chance, then gave her little sister a dubious look, "Yeah, well, somehow Lilly's little adventures always seem to end up getting me in real trouble." Casey then shrugged her shoulders knowingly, realizing full well that it was not all together Lilly's fault, "I really should have been watching her."

"Well," concluded Chance, "she looks fine to me."

Casey took Lilly's hand, "Lilly, you can't just go roaming off like that. I know you don't realize it, but you could get hurt or something."

The emergency over -- the three of them walked back towards the bridge unaware they were being watched by Mole and his henchmen.

8) UNNATURAL ENEMIES & CHARMING STRANGERS

The best way to spend summer vacation days was at Cedar Creek. The best way to spend summer vacation nights was at the Burger Shack Drive-in. For the local kids, it was like a migration of Wildebeest to their next watering hole. Except, in this instance, it was the only stop. Driven by the adolescent instinct to herd...for some, it had become a regular summer's night ritual.

Every adolescent over the age of twelve knew that the Burger Shack was the place where stuff happened and if stuff didn't happen to you, then you got to hear about the stuff that was happening to everybody else. It was like a magnet to every teenager in town.

Sitting in her mom's old Chevy Impala, Casey was finishing off her last bite of hamburger while Mandy slurped down a milkshake. Mandy shrugged, she was in a melancholy mood. "I think Eddie's mad at me. I haven't heard from him in two days."

"Ah," replied Casey, "your dad probably scared him off."

"Not a chance," said Mandy, disagreeing.

"So, what's up?" asked Casey.

"He's probably just being a hardcase...'cause I said we should wait. Hell, it's not like I'm gonna go with him now with only one more year of school left. That'd be stupid, right?"

"Wrong," answered Casey. "That'd be <u>real</u> stupid."

Mandy looked at her somewhat dejected.

"C'mon, Case, you never cut Eddie a break. I know you don't like him much," she said defensively. "But, that's 'cause you don't really know him."

Casey didn't retreat, "I'm just telling it like I see it."

Mandy's attention was suddenly diverted from the subject at hand as a car full of guys pulled into the spot next to them. Her mood changed like quick-silver. An impish grin crossed her

77

face. She nudged Casey as the car load of male teens zeroed in on the two girls.

One look at Casey and Mandy and the guys started whooping and honking the horn. One guy, with a pompadour and a duck tail, leaned out of his window, leering at them.

"Evening, girls. How about a little company?"

Casey was turned off, but Mandy was enjoying the attention.

Seeing that Mandy was up for the game, the driver was encouraged. Sporting a two inch crew cut with a single, long curl down the center of his forehead, he leaned over his buddy on the passenger's side and yelled, "That's right, ladies. We are here to serve your every need. Your wish is our command. Whatever you want, we shall provide."

On cue, his buddies began to whoop and gesture like a pack of baboons.

Mandy giggled, uncontrollably.

Casey looked at him, coolly, "Really?"

He smiled at her and licked his lips in a lascivious gesture, "Just tell us what your sweet, little hearts desire."

"Anything?"

"Oh, yeah, baby, *anything*."

"Good...then get lost."

"Ah, baby, don't be like that."

Mandy squealed as Casey started the car's engine and threw it in reverse. "Let's get out of here," said Casey, having successfully vanquished the driver in his game of words.

Mandy found herself unable to resist giving the guys a final flirtatious smile. She waved good-bye as Casey backed out and started to leave the drive-in.

The commotion had caught the attention of another car parked one row back. It was also filled with guys. As Casey drove the old Chevy out of the drive-in, she did so under the watchful eyes of Mole and his gang. When Mole spotted Casey behind the wheel, he knew his luck had changed.

"Whataya know about that," he said, "it's the chick who took off with that kid."

"What kid?" asked Weasel.

"Whataya mean what kid? The kid that was watchin' us, you idiot!"

"Oh, yeah," Weasel responded, squinting his eyes over the steering wheel to get a better look. "You're right. She's the one that was with that kid."

Bull sat up straight in the back seat and closely watched as they drove by, "That other broad's the one that was with Burkette."

Mole sneered, "Now, ain't that a kick in the head." He looked over at Weasel. "Let's go," he ordered.

Weasel started up the black Pontiac and followed Casey and Mandy out of the drive-in.

***

Both cars headed away from the crowded Burger Shack, down Cedar Grove's main road towards Casey's and Mandy's neighborhood. Oblivious to the threat behind them, Casey and Mandy had rolled their windows down, turned the radio up and were doing a rousing rendition of "You Really Got A Hold On Me." In a moment of inspiration, Mandy stuck her head out of the window into the warm night air and screamed, "Eddie Burkette loves Mandy Banks."

Amused by her friend's antics, Casey grabbed Mandy's blouse and pulled her back into the car. "You nut," she said teasing. "You're gonna get us arrested." They both laughed.

As the two girls pulled into their neighborhood, they saw a sheriff's car parked in front of Mandy's house.

Casey quickly turned off the radio, "What's going on?"

"I don't know," replied Mandy.

Casey pulled up in front of the house and parked. The black Pontiac that had been following them stopped a block away. As the girls got out of their car and went up the walk, Mandy's mother and father, Mr. and Mrs. Banks, came out of the front door of the house. They were being followed by the Sheriff. Mandy could tell by the looks on her parents' faces that something was terribly wrong.

"Mom, what is it? What's happened? Is everything..."

Before she could finish her sentence, Mandy's father exploded in anger. "You want to know what's happened?" he yelled. "I'll tell you what's happened! They found that no good 'boyfriend' of yours tied up in a garbage bag. Somebody dumped him like useless trash up near Cedar Creek! That's...what's happened!!"

The outburst caught the Sheriff completely off guard. Casey was stunned. Mandy was horrified.

She looked desperately at her mother. "Mom, what's he saying?"

"Mandy, honey, somebody...killed Eddie."

Devastated by the reply, Mandy collapsed in her mother's arms, screaming,

"No, Mommie...noooo!"

Casey looked on, helpless, as Mrs. Banks took her distraught daughter inside the house. The Sheriff looked at Mandy's father with disgust.

"May not be any of my business," he said sternly, "but there are a lot of other ways you could have handled that."

Casey watched as the two men glared at each other. Not knowing what else to do, she walked back down the sidewalk and got in her car.

Sickened by the unspeakable turn of events, Casey was completely unaware of anything around her. As she drove away, the black Pontiac once again began to follow. In a state of shock, she drove down the block and around the corner.

She was surprised when she looked up and realized that she had, somehow, arrived in front of her house. It was as if she had driven there on automatic pilot, her mind still dazed from the shocking news.

The Pontiac stopped a short distance away as she pulled into her driveway. She sat for a moment, then opened the car door. Mole watched from the shadows of the black Pontiac as she got out, went up the front steps and opened the front door without using a key.

As she disappeared inside, he sneered to himself, "Gotcha!"

***

Once inside, Casey saw her mother seated on the sofa watching the evening news. Camille glanced up as Casey sat down beside her. They both listened, stunned, as a reporter on the television was doing a story about the murder.

"Authorities say, what links the two murders together is that the body, identified as Jonathan Edward Burkette of Cedar Grove, was found stuffed inside a garbage bag. Another victim... discovered eight months ago...was found similarly dumped in a field in Texarkana. Police are unsure as to what the connection is."

Casey sat dumbfounded as her mother turned down the TV. Camille could only shake her head, "What is this world coming to?" She then looked over at Casey. "Casey...isn't that the young man Mandy's been seeing?" Casey nodded her head and solemnly explained, "I just found out about it when I took Mandy home."

Camille was horrified at the thought of such an evil act, "My dear God, who could believe something like this would ever happen at Cedar Creek."

Casey and her mom sat quietly, not speaking a word. It was as if they had been stunned into silence. For them, the thought of a murder in their small town was all too surreal. An unexpected knock at the front door shook them from their daze. Pulling herself together, Camille went to answer it. As she opened the door, she looked up surprised. It was the Sheriff.

"Excuse me, is your daughter home?" he asked.

Camille looked at him and then back at Casey. Casey shrugged, not knowing why he was there. Camille answered him.

"Yes," she said, "what is it you want?"

"I got her name and address from the father of the Bank's girl. I'm just talking to anyone who knew the Burkette boy."

Camille let him in. Having overheard everything he had said, Casey responded. "I really didn't know him," she explained. She stood up as he entered.

He looked at her, "Casey, right?'"

Casey nodded her head, "yes."

Camille interjected, "If anyone could tell you about Eddie Burkette, it would be Mandy. The two of them were dating."

"Yes, I know," he said, "I'm afraid she's too hysterical to talk just yet. But, she did mention something about last seeing him with a couple of older looking guys. She wasn't able to tell me who they were. She wasn't even sure that she'd ever seen them before."

The Sheriff looked over at Casey and continued, "I understand you were at Cedar Creek the day of the murder."

Camille once more interjected, "We all were."

"Do either of you remember seeing anything suspicious?"

Hearing a sound behind him, the Sheriff turned to look. Standing in the hallway, was Lilly. She was in her pajamas and appeared slightly groggy. Camille looked at Lilly and then back at the officer, "I guess we woke her up. This is my other daughter, Lilly."

Lilly walked over to her mother. As Camille sat down on the couch, Lilly curled up next to her. Casey sat down as well. As the Sheriff took a seat in an old rocking chair near the door, he smiled warmly at Lilly and said cordially, "Hello, Lilly."

He patiently waited for a response.

"Oh...uh, she doesn't talk," explained Camille.

Casey chimed in, "She had an accident before she was born."

The Sheriff nodded, "Well, she's a very pretty little girl."

Lilly was completely unaffected by all of the attention as she sat snug against her mother's side. The Sheriff continued, "As I was saying, did either of you see anything suspicious or unusual that day?" Camille and Casey shook their heads.

"We were having a picnic," Camille said.

"Were you anywhere near the woods?" he inquired.

"Why?"

"That's where the boy's body was found."

Casey interrupted, "Mom."

"What, sweetheart?"

"Those flowers we brought you..."

"What about them?" asked her mother.

"Lilly and I picked them across the bridge, you know, next to the woods. But...but, we didn't see anything."

The Sheriff looked at her, curiously. "Did you go into the woods?"

"Not really," said Casey. "I mean, Lilly kinda roamed off while I was picking the flowers."

"She does that," her mother concurred.

"But, when I went to get her," concluded Casey, "she was fine."

The Sheriff sighed and thought for a minute.

"All right," he said. "Well, if either of you think of anything or remember something, I would appreciate it if you would give me a call." The Sheriff got up to go.

Camille looked over at Casey for help. A very sleepy Lilly was leaning, like a rock, up against her. "Casey, sweetheart, would you put Lilly to bed?"

"Sure, Mom." Casey hopped up and eased her little sister off the sofa and walked her back to the bedroom.

As the Sheriff and Camille walked towards the door, he handed Camille his card. "If you need to get in touch with me...for any reason...just ask for Jeff Colter."

Camille opened the door and took the card from his hand. He then stepped out onto the porch and smiled back at her. "You have very pretty daughters," he said.

"Thank you, I think so."

He looked down for a moment, then raised his head and looked directly at her. "Easy to see where they get it," he said tentatively -- unable to keep his thoughts to himself. Camille was caught off guard. For the first time, she noticed the depth of his blue-gray eyes. She felt a vulnerability as they seemed to peer into her very soul.

She smiled shyly. He smiled back. As he started to leave, she was overwhelmed by feelings of ambivalence. Her mind was telling her no, but her heart was insisting yes. After a moment of awkward silence, her emotions won out and she timidly seized the moment. "If...if you need to reach me for any reason...I've just been promoted to assistant manager at Shey's Restaurant. I'm there most every day. Just ask for Camille Castle."

He was charmed by her sweetness, "I'll do that." He smiled, then began walking down the steps. As Camille closed the door behind him, she sighed unexpectedly to herself. Right out of the blue, it seemed, she had just been hit with another of life's little surprises.

***

For Casey, Saturday mornings at ten o'clock were a fine time. Especially when Lilly had already climbed out of bed, leaving Casey to lavish under the covers, snuggled deep into a pillow. Life was but a dream on mornings like these.

Shifting her body about under the cool sheets, Casey began to stir as she heard the sounds of a lawn mower creeping into her subconscious. Lingering a moment longer in a sleepy haze, she managed to swing both legs over the side of the bed and sit up. She quickly shielded her eyes, allowing them to adjust to the morning sun that filtered into the room.

Still groggy, she took a good, long stretch, yawned and looked out of her bedroom window. She gasped ever so slightly.

Chance was busy mowing his grandmother's lawn. He wore only shorts with a towel draped around his neck. His upper body gleamed brightly as it soaked up the warm rays of the rising sun. He stopped momentarily to towel-off the perspiration that dripped from his muscular shoulders down the curve of his back.

Mrs. Eberworth's Labrador Retriever, Sport, bounced around him, barking. Chance playfully snapped the towel at

Sport before returning it to his neck. The dog wagged its tail and barked, enjoying the attention.

Mesmerized, Casey lingered for a moment, taking in the view. Without warning, sudden and unexpected feelings began to stir deep within her young body. She was awash in a wave of warm, tingling sensations that seemed to flow through her -- awakening her senses. But, the moment was not to last. Unknowingly, her mother suddenly popped her head in the door, abruptly breaking the spell that had been cast upon her daughter.

"Honey, Lilly's been perched in the rocking chair by the door for the last hour. I think she wants to go out. Would you mind?" she asked.

When she turned to look at her mother, what was left of Casey's lingering emotions quickly disappeared, bursting in mid-air like fragile soap bubbles on a windy day. As she allowed them to evaporate into nothingness, she yawned, took another good stretch, then answered.

"Sure, Mom. I'll be right there."

***

Minutes later, Casey entered the living room to find Lilly impatiently standing, primed and ready, at the front door. Casey looked over at her and grinned.

"Hey, Kiddo, what's the rush?"

She went over and sat Lilly back down in the rocking chair as her mom called from the kitchen, "Sweetie, I made you some toast. You want eggs or oatmeal?"

Casey gave Lilly a quick kiss on the cheek and said, "I'll be right back."

She went into the kitchen and poured herself some milk and chomped down on a piece of toast her mom had prepared.

"What'll it be?" asked Camille, waiting to take Casey's breakfast order.

"No time, Mom. Lilly's got me on a tight schedule. You oughta see her. She is so ready to go."

"Where you girls going?"

"I think we'll walk down to the school playground. Hang out there a while. You know how she loves to get out and see stuff."

"That she does," said her mother. "You girls be careful."

Casey gulped down her milk, rinsed out the glass and then went to get Lilly. Lilly was back up, once again standing by the door.

Casey looked at her, "All right, already, I'm coming."

The two girls headed out of the front door for their adventure.

*＊＊

Clover Elementary School was one place that just about everybody in Cedar Grove had in common. If a body didn't go there as a kid, then they probably had a kid or two who went there now. It was a safe place filled with lots of memories and most of Cedar Groves' younger citizens -- grades one through six. Like most elementary schools in the summer time, its playgrounds were used by just about anybody who wanted to enjoy them.

That day was no exception. A man and his boys were hitting balls on the elementary school's baseball mound. The father lobbed a slow pitch to his younger son as his older boy played short stop. The kid took a swing and hit a long foul ball. The ball rolled to a stop near the swings where Casey and Lilly were playing. Casey picked up the ball and tossed it to the older boy. As the ball landed with a smack in the palm of his glove, the kid yelled back, "Hey, good arm." Casey smiled to herself. She always did have a good right arm.

Having done her bit to keep their practice session going, she returned to Lilly and the swings. Lilly held on tightly as Casey once again pushed the swing into the air. Lilly found it exhilarating and was enjoying her outing immensely. The higher she went, the brighter she smiled. Casey loved hearing her joyful giggles, though she was careful never to let the swing fly too high.

Across from the school, a dirty, black Pontiac sat unnoticed on a neighborhood side street. Inside, its occupants sat patiently watching the activity on the playground. Suddenly, there was an ominous boom. A loud clap of thunder was followed by yet another low rumbling off in the distance.

Casey looked up as the wind began to pick up. The dark clouds off on the horizon appeared to be rolling in their direction.

"Oh-oh. Looks like we're going to have to cut this short," she said slowing the swing to a halt. As a light sprinkle began to fall around them, Casey attempted to pull a reluctant Lilly off of the swing.

"Sorry, Lilly, but we gotta get home."

Casey gave her one more tug. This time, Lilly didn't resist. As the wind began to whirl in small gusts around them, she noticed that the man and his boys had also decided to give it up and were piling themselves and their gear into a nearby stationwagon.

*****

As Casey and Lilly began their trek home, the black Pontiac pulled away from the curb and slowly began to follow them. The rain had started to come down harder. Tugging at Lilly, Casey did her best to hurry her along, but she quickly realized the inevitable.

"Oh man, we're gonna get drenched."

The girls made their way as quickly as they could into the neighborhood.

The Pontiac continued to follow. A huge bolt of lightning cracked across the sky and, as if the bottom had dropped out, the rain began to pour down. Casey looked at Lilly. She was soaked to the skin and was beginning to shiver slightly.

"Man, Lilly, if you catch a cold, Mama's gonna kill me. C'mon, we gotta get you out of this rain."

Casey hurried Lilly onto the front steps of a nearby house. Lilly sat down on the steps in a small huddle with her back against the wall.   Casey rang the doorbell and said with assurance, "I'll call home. Have Mama come pick us up."

She rang the bell again. There was no answer. She opened the outer screen door, blocking Lilly between it and the wall. She then knocked HARD on the large, wooden front door. She listened carefully for signs of movement inside. After a moment, she looked down at Lilly and gave her a shrug.

"Guess it's not our lucky day."

9)   CLOSE ENCOUNTERS

Less than a half block away, the black Pontiac eased down a street that directly faced the house and parked. It sat there like a predator stalking it prey, its three occupants watching and waiting.

Determined, Casey was not about to give up her quest to get to a phone. Once again, she opened the screen and knocked hard on the large, wooden front door. She looked down at Lilly who was still shivering in her wet clothes as she huddled against the wall. Clearly, it was time for Casey to take matters into own hands. She reached out and gripped the door knob, giving it a good twist. To her amazement, it turned. She quickly released it.

"It's open! Guess they're in the garage or on the back porch or something," she said, encouraged.

Reaching behind the screen, she took Lilly's hand and pulled her to her feet, "C'mon, doll, we'll ask them if we can use the phone."

She gave the doorbell one more try. She heard a rustling sound. Then a big thump. Relieved, she smiled at Lilly, "All right. I think I hear somebody."

Certain that there was somebody in the house who knew she was out there, she waited patiently for a moment. She could clearly hear noises inside, but no one was responding. Frustrated, Casey reached for the front door knob again.

Turning it slowly, she opened the large, wooden door and then leaned in slightly and called out, "Hello. Is any body..."

Before Casey could utter another word, she caught a glimpse of what appeared to be a creature-possessed moving swiftly through the shadows inside the house. An immediate sense of danger sent a shiver down her spine. Panicked, she quickly ducked backwards as a huge blur of *gnashing white fangs attached to a snarling, growling massive black face* came flying through the air directly at her. With her heart bursting with fear, she had no time to think. Acting on pure adrenaline, she barely managed to slam the outer screen door shut as the angry beast rammed into it. In a wild, savage frenzy, the large dog repeatedly gouged its face hard up against the screen straining it outwards as it continued barking and snarling at the two intruders.

Petrified, Casey leaned forward with all of her might against the screen door, holding it shut for dear life. Practically face to face with the animal, she watched in horror as the huge Doberman continued banging its massive body against the screen, almost knocking it open.

Startled at the sight of the huge animal, little Lilly looked up at her sister...then back at the barking Doberman...and promptly got up to leave. Aghast, Casey made a desperate grab with one arm, barely catching Lilly by the shirttail. Sensing the vulnerability of the situation, the dog slammed its body even harder into the screen.

Struggling to hold the door shut, Casey braced her back against it as she was simultaneously being pulled in the opposite direction by a very determined Lilly. Lilly was ready to leave, heading off -- *alone if necessary* -- to who knows where. To Casey, the thought of Lilly roaming off on her own was considerably more frightening than the dog.

So, there she stood, caught between the proverbial rock and a hard place. Except this time, the hard place had teeth and was ramming itself non-stop against her back. She knew she had one shot, and one shot only, at keeping the situation from going from really bad to may not live to talk about it.

In what seemed like a fraction of a second, Casey made her move. As Lilly pulled forward to make good her escape, Casey gave her one swift yank backwards causing Lilly to lose her balance. As Lilly tumbled down onto the steps, the momentum of the fall forced Casey forward, away from the screen door, allowing it to open slightly.

Seeing daylight between the door and the frame, the dog quickly jammed its nose into the crack. It suddenly yelped and jumped back startled as Casey shifted balance and slammed the full weight of her body back up against the door. Stung by the pinch of the slamming door on the tip of its nose, the enraged dog barked even more fiercely as Casey eased Lilly back onto the porch out of the pouring rain.

"Lilly!" she insisted, "you've got to sit down. We...we can't go yet."

As Lilly obediently sat down with her back to the wall, the dog once again rammed its large body against the screen, snarling and baring its teeth. Casey could see the screen bulging outward. It was starting to give way from the large dog's repeated impacts. Badly shaken by this unthinkable turn of events, Casey looked down at a terrified Lilly, then at the noisy, barking dog. Totally frustrated and frightened out of her wits, she screamed at the dog.

"Shut up!! You dumb animal. You nearly scared the hell outta me!!!"

Suddenly confronted by overt, aggressive behavior, the dog abruptly stopped barking, let out a small whine and looked at her. Casey stood there, equally amazed at the dog's reaction. The two of them eyed each other for a moment. The dog let out another low whine. Not wanting to lose the sudden advantage of the upper hand, Casey quickly decided to try a different tact. With a new found authority and in her most commanding voice, she ordered the dog, "Get back. You hear me? Get back into the house!"

The dog growled -- but, stepped back a little.

"That's right...that's what I said. Get back into the house!"

The dog looked at her for a second and then backed away from the screen door. Casey was heartened, but still watched carefully as the dog roamed around, all the while putting distance between itself and the door.

"That's a good dog," she said, trying to maintain her cool.

Casey watched as the dog sat down on a throw rug. It continued eyeing her as closely as she was eyeing it. With her

91

courage wearing thin, Casey decided it was time to make her move. She began to very slowly open the screen door. As she was doing so, the dog growled ever so slightly, making a guttural sound deep in its throat. Not to be deterred, Casey continued to carefully reach inside, slowly stretching her hand towards the knob of the big, wooden door. As if finally figuring out what she was up to, the big dog quickly stood up, but it was too late.

With her last ounce of courage, Casey made a grab for the knob. As she was swinging the door shut, the big dog again became enraged and made a desperate leap across the room, snarling ferociously. It was a serious miscalculation. With teeth gnashing, it flew head first, with a loud THUNK into the BACK of the thick, wooden door.

Hoping with all of her might that it would provide additional protection, Casey hurriedly slammed the outer screen door shut as well. She then collapsed into a heap on to the porch. Breathing heavily and trying to catch her breath, she looked over at Lilly.

"What do you think...we had enough excitement for today?"

Lilly got up determined to go this time. Casey took her by the hand and headed down the steps, "I'm with you, Kiddo." She glanced up at the sky, "Well, at least the rain let up."

Casey looked up the street just in time to see the black Pontiac start to ease towards them. She watched curiously, realizing there was something familiar about it. As the Pontiac picked up speed and headed towards them, another car suddenly passed by. The other car stopped, then backed up, pulling up to the curb next to the girls.

The car's passenger side door swung open and Chance smiled up at Casey, "You look like you could use a ride."

Casey looked in at him, concerned, "We're soaked. Your car will be a mess."

"Won't be the first time," he said. "C'mon, hop in."

With that, Casey smiled and helped Lilly into the front seat. She slid in beside her, closing the door.

Inside the black Pontiac, a flustered Weasel looked over at Mole while Chance's car pulled away from the curb, "She's gettin' away. What the hell we gonna do now?"

Mole just smirked, "Girl ain't going nowhere we can't find her."

The three goons watched as Chance and the two girls drove off down the street.

***

Minutes later, Chance pulled his car into the driveway at Casey's house. Getting out quickly, he hurried around the car to open Casey's door. By the time he got there, Casey had already climbed out. But, Lilly had other plans. She had slipped behind the wheel, in the driver's seat, and was happily steering away. It was as if, in her little head, she was off on her own holiday -- driving down the road to wherever it would take her. Chance and Casey looked in at her.

"She likes to drive," Casey explained. "Well, not drive. But, you know, act like it. She's been doing it since she was little."

Casey started to reach inside the car. "I'll get her."

Chance touched her on the shoulder, "Hey...don't worry about it. I don't mind. I mean, as long as she kicks in for the gas." He smiled.

Casey laughed, "Sure, no problem...she's good for it."

Leaving Lilly to her road trip, the two of them walked over to the front porch and sat down. A sudden silence richly filled the rarefied air that now seemed to encircle them. Aware of their growing attraction to one another, they both sat awkwardly for a moment unsure of how to proceed, much less conquer, the new and fertile ground of their budding relationship. After what seemed like an eternity, Casey broke the silence and blurted out, "How's your grandmother doing?"

Chance hesitated at first, then replied, "Better."

"I sure would like to see her," continued Casey, not noticing his reticence.

"Mom says that she's still not letting anyone visit...she didn't even really tell me what was wrong with her."

Chance was uneasy with her inquiry. "It's kind of a private matter."

"Well, tell her as soon as she's ready, I want to come see her. Okay?" Chance gave her a sort of half-cocked smile and nodded a half-hearted, "okay."

Suddenly, they were both distracted by the sound of crunching gravel. They looked up just in time to see Lilly and Chance's car drifting slowly backwards, down the driveway, towards the street.

"Oh my God!" exclaimed Casey. "She must have slipped it in gear."

They both jumped to their feet and ran after the car. Lilly was happily steering away as the car continued down the driveway into the street.

Casey and Chance could only watch as it made its way across the street to the other side. They both grimaced and let out a small gasp as the back wheels bounced off the opposite curb, just inches from the front of a neighbor's car. The car rolled forward to a slow stop -- stretching across both lanes of traffic.

Casey and Chance rushed up to the car and saw Lilly, still determinedly, turning the steering wheel. It had been a good trip, but it was evident she still wanted more. Seeing that no damage was done, Chance looked through the window and smiled at Lilly. "Hey, kid, nobody said anything about a joy ride."

Casey was mortified. She opened the door and helped Lilly out, all the while apologizing to Chance, "I'm really sorry. I...I should have..."

He cut her off. "Hey, I always say no harm, no foul."

"She doesn't really mean to do this kind of stuff," Casey tried to explain. "It's just that she doesn't know any better."

"Listen," he said, "when I was her age, I did the same thing. Except, I backed into my granddaddy's fishing boat."

"You didn't?"

"Oh yeah. I slipped his old Buick in gear and, within seconds, turned that right hull into kindling wood. First time I ever saw grand dad turn purple."

They both laughed.

"So, the way I figure it," he said, "she didn't do that bad, did she?"

Casey looked at him warmly. "I'd say...Lilly's got herself a pretty good defense lawyer."

Chance grinned, "Guilty as charged." He quickly put up his hands defensively and teased, "Me...not my client."

He looked at her and smiled, broadly. She smiled back. They both sensed it, a brief stirring of the heart, causing them both to catch their breath as it momentarily seemed to escape them.

Taking Lilly by the hand, Casey was first to falter from the moment, "I think I'd better get her in. Thanks for the ride."

"Anytime," he said, meaning it. "Catch you later, huh?'

"Yeah, later," replied Casey.

Chance looked at Lilly, "Bye, Lilly."

Casey and Lilly watched as Chance got into his car and pulled away. Once he was out of earshot, Casey looked at Lilly and queried out loud, "Whataya think? Wow...huh?"

But, her musing was short lived as reality set in.

"Oh-oh! We better get going. I bet Mama's startin' to worry."

Walking with Lilly up the sidewalk towards the house, Casey jolted to a sudden stop. "Oh, and Lilly, about your little 'joy ride,' I won't mention it if you don't, okay? And, about that dog thing...I don't even wanna begin to think of how to explain that."

With no apparent objections from Lilly, the two sisters disappeared inside the house.

10)   WHOSE NIGHTMARE IS IT, ANYWAY?

On the other side of town, things were not going so swimmingly. Mandy's world was in a tailspin. She was at the counter of a convenience store trying to buy a six pack of beer which she was clinging to, holding it securely against her side. She had already had one beer too many, her speech was slurred and she looked like hell.

Mandy was wearing her favorite outfit, yellow pedal-pushers and a halter top with a pattern of yellow and white daisies. She had always liked the way the yellow and white set off her bright, red hair, highlighting its luminous curls. Eddie always said it made her look like one of those young, sexy movie starlets.

But, that day, the bright coloring of her clothing was, if anything, a vivid contradiction. The sunny yellow and white daisies, splashed across the skimpy scrap of material that was her halter top, were in sharp contrast to her true disposition. At the moment, she was feeling very raw and very empty inside. A sour feeling in the pit of her stomach was telling her life had taken a wrong turn.

But, Mandy was too far gone to realize that if she wasn't careful, this might be the first of many such pit falls. Seventeen was too young an age for a girl like Mandy to understand that she was flirting with a harsher side of life from which even pretty, young girls are not immune. A few more wrong steps could send her plummeting downward on a life-long slide that would eventually leave her on the bottom looking up.

As scary as that prospect was, at that moment Mandy really didn't give a damn. All she knew was that she had lost Eddie and she was desperate to escape the pain.

She stood there stubbornly in front of the counter. Come what may, she fully intended to leave the store with a six pack of beer. She was ready for a stand-off as she waved her money in front of the clerk and adamantly proclaimed, "I don't care if you take the money or not, I'm not leavin' without this beer!"

The store's clerk was just as adamant she wasn't getting it. His patience worn, he was practically yelling at her, "I told you, I'm not sellin' you any beer. You're under age."

Weaving slightly, Mandy caught her balance, defiantly slammed the money down on the counter and yelled, "Says who?!"

"Says me," he replied equally defiant, "I don't know where you got your first couple of rounds, but you ain't gettin' any here." He shoved her money back at her.

As the confrontation continued, three new customers entered the store unnoticed. It was Mole, Weasel and Bull. They could hear the clerk yelling.

"Take your money and get out of here! I don't need this kinda trouble."

His curiosity piqued by the ruckus, Weasel squinted his eyes to see what was going on. He spotted Mandy. He nudged Mole in the side, pointed in Mandy's direction and said, "Hey, Mole, Mole...take look at this."

Mole and Bull looked in the direction Weasel was staring. Bull instantly recognized Mandy

"Well, whataya know," commented Bull, "that's the babe that was gettin' all hot'n bothered with Burkette."

Mole quickly raised his hand to silence them both, then carefully watched Mandy for a moment. It was evident to him that she had been drinking. He motioned to Weasel and Bull to get lost. Without hesitation, Bull and Weasel did as they were instructed and hastily exited the store.

As Mandy continued to argue with the clerk, Mole went over, stood beside her at the counter and took out some money. Irritated at his apparent brashness, Mandy snarled at him, "Hey, pal, I was here first, take a hike."

Mole smirked and reached over for the six pack. Forcing it out of her hands, he slammed it down on the counter and leaned one arm on top if it.

"Why don't you wait outside, little girl. I got a purchase to make."

Mandy looked at the clerk and then back at Mole in disbelief. "Give me that!" she yelled as she tried unsuccessfully to pry the beer away from Mole. Realizing she was outnumbered, she threw up her hands in disgust and left the store in a huff.

Mole tossed his money down on the counter and gave the clerk a threatening look. Not wanting anymore trouble than he had already had, the clerk shrugged his shoulders and took it. Mole smirked, picked up the beer and began to walk out of the store. Before he got to the door, he turned around, cocked his thumb backwards like he was holding a gun, pointed his finger at the leery clerk and pretended to fire. He laughed as the clerk winced. Mole exited through the front door, still laughing. The clerk stood behind the counter, motionless -- just grateful to be rid of him.

***

Outside in the convenience store's parking lot, Mandy waited nervously for Mole to come out of the door. She had braced herself up against the door of the dirty black Pontiac for support. She was too far out of it to notice that its grime had already imbedded itself into her yellow pedal-pushers like a bad omen. Seeing her waiting, Mole held the beer high over his head as if it were a victory prize.

"Hey, Baby...this what you wanted?"

Seeing the beer, Mandy stumbled towards him in anticipation, "Yeah...thanks."

As she stretched out her hand for it, he yanked the beer out of her reach, laughing. "Not so fast, sweet thing. Whataya say, you and me...we go for a ride. "

Mandy looked at him, disgusted. "I don't want any of your crap, okay? I just want the beer."

"C'mon, sugar, I did you a favor. The least you can do is share one with me." He continued to coax her, "We'll take a spin. Get some fresh air." He eyed her closely, "You sure as hell look like you could use it."

Mandy grabbed for one of the beers. He caught her as she lost her balance. Straightening herself up, she brushed her hair back off of her face.

"Don't tell me what I need, creep."

Mole backed off a little, "No problem, we'll take a little ride and you can tell me, okay?" He opened the passenger side door for her.

"C'mon...I got an opener in the car."

Mandy looked at him, bleary-eyed. "Fine...whatever. I'm thirsty."

Mole grinned and helped Mandy into the black Pontiac. He quickly got in and opened them both a beer. He handed one to her. Mandy grabbed it and gulped it down as if she were dying of thirst. Mole watched her and threw back his head, laughing.

"What the hell's so funny?" she demanded.

Feigning an uncustomary timidity, he said sheepishly, "Nothin'. Nothin'. Just looks like you got yourself a mighty big thirst, that's all."

"Maybe I do, what's it to you?" she said, gulping down another swig of beer.

"All I'm sayin' is that you ain't gotta sweat it, darlin'," he answered her, "'cause there's always plenty more where this came from."

As if to reassure her, Mole placed the remaining six pack securely in her lap. He watched as she clung to it. Once again, laughing out loud, he pulled out of the parking lot onto the street with his tires squealing. Out of the corner of his eye he spotted Bull and Weasel as they waited haplessly across the street in front of a hardware store for further instructions. Stomping on the gas, he sped past them and laughed even harder.

***

Several miles down the road, Mandy was feeling no pain as she finished off another beer. She and Mole soon found themselves on the outskirts of Cedar Grove, on the old highway. Except for the black Pontiac, the highway was all but abandoned. The only sign of civilization was an old gas station that had been shut-down for years -- it's rusted pumps still standing as monuments to better days. With no other cars in sight, Mole sped recklessly down the center of the old road, pushing the car to its limits.

Just beyond the old gas station, the speeding car suddenly made a sharp turn, fishtailed off the main road and traveled up a graveled driveway. A short distance farther, Mole raced the black Pontiac into the parking lot of an old abandoned beer joint. A large sign on the roof, covered in dried and cracking paint, identified the place as Cutahey's Lounge.

Cutahey's sat isolated on a small hill in the middle of a wooded area. The only way in and out of its dirt parking area was the graveled road that slanted downward, leading back out to the old highway. The old bar's windows were securely boarded up even though the sign on top still extended the greeting: "Welcome to Cutahey's Lounge." It was clearly an invitation whose time had run out a long time ago.

The car suddenly lurched to a stop. Mole got out. He then went around to the passenger's side and pulled an inebriated Mandy out of the car.

"C'mon, Baby. I got something I think you're gonna like."

Mandy no longer resisted and slid out of the car -- still clinging to her remaining beers for comfort.

***

Once inside Cutahey's Lounge, Mole flipped on a light as Mandy stumbled through the door. Mandy looked around and took another swig of her beer.

"Where the hell are we?" she asked.

"Our own secret hideaway. It's where I work and where I play."

It was evident that the old bar had seen better days -- not that it had ever been much to brag about, not even in its heyday. It consisted basically of a large rectangular room with a few remaining tables and chairs stacked on top of one another in a corner. A number of the chairs appeared to be broken -- apparently from one brawl too many.

Seven bar stools managed to remain positioned in front of the bar itself, though several of their bolts had come loose from the rotting floor. Three of the bar stools' thick, green naugahide seat covers had cracked. Rusty-orange colored stuffing oozed out of every available crevice and spilled over the sides as dried bits of foam littered the floor below. The entire place had a thick, musty smell from the layer of dust that coated everything.

It ain't the Taj Mahal," cracked Mole, "but for the time being, it's all I need to get by."

Mole took Mandy by the arm and led her over to an old sofa that had been placed in the middle of the floor, facing the bar. The sofa, with its large misshapen cushions and dark turquoise and gold covering appeared to be on its last legs. It had been scavenged from the side of the road somewhere. It was one of the few things in the room that wasn't covered with dust. He sat her down on it.

"Now, you just sit right here and make yourself comfortable, sweet thing. It's time for you and me to get to know each other. Whataya say, huh?"

Smiling, he leaned down and tried to kiss her on the side of the neck. In her stupor, Mandy pushed him away.

"Cut it out! I don't want...that."

He stepped back and laughed as she fell drowsily back onto the sofa.

"Hey, whatever, sweetheart. You just relax, 'cause 'ol Mole is gonna bring you something you do want. Then, we'll have a little talk about Eddie, okay?"

"Eddie?" Mandy looked up bleary-eyed, "What do you know about Eddie?"

Ignoring her, Mole left her lying on the sofa as he went behind the bar. Reaching under the counter, he pulled out a white bag of powder and a large spoon. He scooped out a spoon full of the white substance, pulled a cigarette lighter out of his front pocket and held it under the spoon. As he heated the white powdery substance, Mandy continued to babble to herself.

"Eddie loved me. We were going away together. He had it all planned." Mole went back over to Mandy, "Yeah, sweetheart, he was a real prince."

She looked up. She saw that he had a hypodermic needle clenched sideways between his teeth. She watched drowsily as he tied a dirty rag around her upper arm.

"What are you doin'?"

She pulled her arm away in a reflex action and cowered back into the sofa.

"Hey, now. Take it easy, baby. This is gonna make you feel better."

Mole stretched Mandy's arm out and took the hypodermic from between his teeth.

She flinched as he injected her with it.

"That's it. Easy now," he cautioned. "Just lay back. It's time for you to take a ride on the big white horse."

As the drug took hold, Mandy's body became limp and she began to mellow out even more. "He really loved me...you know?"

"Yeah, little girl, that's what I'm countin' on."

Mandy eased back, sinking deep into the sofa cushions as she slipped into semi-consciousness under the effects of the drug and the alcohol.

***

Supper time in a small town like Cedar Grove usually started around four in the afternoon and lasted until nobody was hungry. It was a time that found folks either at home around the dinner table or downtown at one of the local eateries.

It was early evening when a sheriff's car pulled up into a parking space in front of Shey's Restaurant. Located in the center of town, Shey's was a family style restaurant that had been around as long as any of the locals could remember. Sheriff Jeff Colter got out of the patrol car and went inside.

He could see that the restaurant was fairly busy. He took off his hat and checked out the room more closely. He looked around slowly. He didn't see what he was looking for.

Seeing him standing there, a waitress approached him and smiled. She pointed to the other side of the dining area, "There's a table over there, if you'd like."

"Uh...no, thank you, he said, disappointed. "I think I'll just..."

Suddenly, he saw her. Coming out of a back office was Camille. He looked at the waitress. "Excuse me, will you?" As he stepped around the waitress, Camille looked over and saw him. Surprised, she smiled. He quickly walked over to her.

"Evening, Mrs. Castle."

"Sheriff Colter. How nice to see you. You out on some kind of investigation?"

He smiled at her, awkwardly, "You might say that."

He noticed that her purse was hanging over her shoulder. "You...you leaving?"

"Yes," she answered, "I just got off."

"Great. I mean...uh, would you like to get a bite to eat? Or, maybe a cup of coffee. That is, if...if you're not hungry."

Camille blushed. She looked around the restaurant. She saw two of the waitresses staring at them. She lowered her voice, "Maybe we should go some place where we'll attract a little less attention?"

Colter looked over and saw the waitresses staring. He nodded his "okay."

"But, first," said Camille, "I need to call home. Let the girls know I'll be running late."

She motioned for him to follow her into the office. Without hesitation, he did so. Once inside, he shut the door behind them. Suddenly, Camille turned and looked up at him. She took a deep breath as if she were getting her wits about her.

She then said hesitantly, "I'm sorry. Maybe...this isn't such a good idea..."

Taken aback by her sudden change of heart, he could only stammer, "Why...why not?"

Camille hesitated, taking a moment to gather her thoughts. She leaned awkwardly against the front of her desk for support.

"Look," she said with a great uncertainty, "I don't know if this is being presumptuous or not. And, I apologize if it is...but, there's something I gotta make clear. I'm flattered by your interest. I am. But, I don't have time to be somebody's passing fancy here..."

"Camille..."

"I mean," she continued, "I don't have that kind of luxury...and, if I did, I wouldn't...

Once more he interrupted, "Camille."

The calmness in his voice stopped her. She looked at him. He went over to her.

"That's not the way it is," he explained to her gently. "I'm not sure what this is...but you're nobody's 'passing fancy.'"

She stared at him. Part of her remained uncertain, but the other part wanted very badly to believe him. She looked at him, standing there tall and self-assured in his neatly pressed uniform.

"What makes you so brave?" she asked.

"What makes you think I am?"

"Most men make a beeline for the door when they find out I have two daughters. Especially...Lilly."

"I'm not most men."

"Maybe you're not," she said, half-hoping.

"Besides," he continued, "I've already met your girls. And, from what I can see, those two bring out the best in you. Especially, Lilly."

Touched by his gentleness, she looked at him shyly and smiled.

"In that case," she said, still stumbling over her emotions, "I suppose grabbing a bite somewhere...won't do much harm."

"Not a bit," he assured her.

She smiled sweetly at him. It was obvious that her warmth captivated him. His eyes seemed to soften at the very sight of her. He watched as she went over, picked up the phone and dialed.

***

Back at the house, Casey was busy in front of the bathroom mirror brushing her hair up off of her neck into a pony tail when she heard the phone ringing. She quickly picked up a large barrette from the side of the sink. She grimaced to herself at the insistent ringing of the phone and hurriedly clipped the barrette into her hair. Pulling herself away from the mirror, she scurried out of the bathroom into the small hallway to answer it. She picked up the receiver and said in a matter-of-fact tone, "Hello."

Hearing her mother's voice, she beamed, "Hi, Mom."

Casey listened, idly fiddling with the phone cord, twisting it slowly around her index finger. "Yeah, Mom, she's fine. Don't worry about it." She quickly added, "Just don't work too late, okay?"

She listened again, this time snapping the phone cord back and forth like a rubber band. Somewhat impetuously, she raised her eyebrows and emphatically insisted into the phone, "Mom...we'll be fine. We love you, too...okay?"

As soon as Casey hung up the phone, it rang again.

Casey answered it, "Hello." She listened. "No, Mrs. Banks, Mandy's not here." A look of concern briefly crossed her face. "Yes, ma'am. If I see her, I'll tell her you're looking for her."

Before she could put the receiver down, she heard a knock at the front door. Curious, she quickly placed the phone's receiver back in its cradle, walked over to the living room window and peeked out through the blinds. Astonished at the sight, she quickly went to the door and opened it. Standing on the front steps was Mandy. She was barely able to stay on her feet.

Casey reached out to steady her friend, "Mandy!"

She took one of Mandy's arms to help her inside. Casey then heard what sounded like someone gunning an engine. Steadying her friend, she took a moment to look up, barely catching a glimpse of the back end of a black car as it pulled away from the curb and disappeared.

Once Mandy was safely inside, she closed the door, took her over to the sofa and sat down beside her. She grimaced slightly.

"God, Mandy, you smell like a brewery."

All Mandy could do was groan, "Casey, I don't feel so good."

Casey could clearly see her point. "Jimini, Mandy, you don't look so good either. I mean...you know, you're a little green around the gills."

"I think I'm gonna be sick," Mandy moaned turning a paler shade of pale.

"Your mom just called," Casey informed her.

"My mom?"

"Yeah. She's been looking for you. I think she's worried. You want me to have her come pick you up?"

"No...no," Mandy cried out, strenuously objecting to Casey's suggestion, "if my dad sees me like this, he'll kill me." She leaned back on the sofa, "I...I just want to lie down for a little while, okay?"

"Sure," said Casey. She watched as Mandy collapsed back into the cushions.

"Who was that who dropped you off?" Casey asked curiously.

"I don't know. Some friend of Eddie's. He's got this place. He gave me something to make me feel better...but, I don't."

Mandy started to cry. "I need Eddie. He was going to take care of me. Now...it's over! It's all over!"

Mandy sobbed loudly. Casey pulled her friend close and brushed her hair off her face.

"Shss, shss, I know it's been really terrible," she said trying to calm her. "Pretty soon...I mean, in time, maybe it won't hurt so bad. Besides, Mandy, it's not over. You're barely getting started with your life."

"You don't understand, my dad is gonna kill me."

"No, he's not. Mandy, he's not going to hurt you. He was just mad at you. He was just..." Casey struggled to find the right word... "disappointed, that's all."

Mandy's tears seemed more uncontrollable, "You don't understand."

Casey was even more insistent, "I'm telling you, he's going to get over it."

"No...he's not."

"Yes, he is."

"No, he's not!" she practically screamed.

Her tears flowing like water, Mandy completely broke down and blurted out the totally unexpected.

"I'm pregnant!" she wailed.

Stunned, the revelation hit Casey like a brick, leaving her virtually speechless.

"Wha..what?"

"Promise me, promise me you won't tell anyone," Mandy pleaded anxiously. "Please, Casey, I need your help," she bellowed.

Completely overwhelmed, Casey grappled with her emotions as her thoughts began to collide with one another. She could barely hear her own voice as the first words came out of her mouth, "Mandy, you have to tell your parents."

"I can't! Eddie's gone! I can't have this baby. You have to help me!"

Casey was beginning to feel as desperate as her friend. "Okay, okay," she said, conceding, "I'll call your mom, tell her you're staying overnight."

Relieved, Mandy once again broke down and cried on Casey's shoulder. Sitting there saddened and confused, Casey realized there was nothing she could do but bear witness as life delivered one of its harsh consequences to her best friend. It was, of course, not the first time she had been confronted by an unchangeable reality. Nonetheless, she didn't feel good about it. She didn't feel good about it at all. She knew from experience that sometimes it's hard to imagine the unimaginable, until it's staring you right in the face. And, there it was, bigger than life - - once again looking Casey right in the eye.

***

The following morning arrived far too early. Casey could hear her mom busily preparing breakfast as she ambled into the dining room in her robe and pajamas. She peered into the small kitchen.

"Mornin', Mom."

"Mornin', Doll."

Camille watched as Casey sleepily slumped down at the table, then said casually, "Casey, you didn't tell me Mandy was staying over. I saw her bunked out on the floor last night when I looked in on you girls."

Casey barely looked up, "Yeah. It was kinda sudden."

"Everything okay?" asked her mother.

"Yeah." Casey rubbed her face in her hands and looked down, forlorn, at the table. She hated lying to her mother. She decided to fess-up.

"Uh...no. Actually, Mom...she'd had a couple of beers and she was, you know...afraid to go home." She sighed to herself. Well, at least a half truth was better than no truth. Concerned, Camille came out of the kitchen.

"Has she done this before?" asked her mom.

"No. I mean, she and Eddie used to down a few. But, I never saw her this bad."

Camille sat down at the table and looked earnestly at her daughter. "Honey, I don't think that covering for her is such a good idea. It's like condoning it...and that can only make it worse. You don't want to encourage that kind of behavior."

"Mom, I didn't encourage her."

"I know, sweetheart. But, going along with her makes her think it's all right. This is really between Mandy and her parents. How are they going to help her, if they don't know? You understand what I'm saying?"

Casey gave her Mother a soulful look. "Yeah, Mom, I know."

They both turned around when they heard Mandy walk into the room.

She was unkempt and disheveled having slept in her clothes all night.

"Good morning, Mandy," said Camille.

"Hello, Mrs. Castle," she responded.

"Would you like some breakfast?" Camille offered.

"No, I gotta go. I don't feel so good," she said as she headed for the door. Casey got up and followed Mandy to the front door. As they stepped out onto the front porch, Mandy appeared anxious.

"You didn't tell her, did you?"

"No. I didn't tell her," Casey quickly answered.

Mandy seemed momentarily relieved. Casey looked at her friend. Her mom's words weighed heavily on her mind. She knew she had to do the right thing. Sighing heavily, she said, "Mandy, you're going to have to tell your mom and dad."

Mandy was nonplused. Feeling the effects of her hangover, she barely caught her breath as she snorted sarcastically, "Yeah, right...I'll get back to you on that one."

Without further comment, Mandy rubbed her face in her hands and wearily made her way down the front steps. As she walked slowly across the yard towards the street, Casey called after her, "You want me to drive you home?"

Shaking her head in disgust, Mandy blew her off, "Oh, please. Don't do me any favors."

Casey was distraught, "Mandy...!?"

Mandy looked back at her, "I thought you'd understand. But, you just don't get it, do you? None of it is worth it without Eddie." She turned and faced Casey as tears welled up in her eyes, "I mean, what the hell...even you won't let me catch a break."

Helpless, Casey watched as her friend walked away. Camille came to the door and stood behind her daughter and asked, "She okay?"

"Not really," replied Casey.

They both stood in the doorway, their thoughts swept away by the pain of someone they both cared about. As Casey's eyes began to brim with tears, Camille put her arm around her daughter's waist and stood next to her without saying a word.

Casey took a couple of deep breaths. She felt comforted by the silence of her mother's non-judgmental support.

After a moment, Camille gave her a reassuring hug and then said, "Sweetheart, I want you to drive me to work after breakfast."

"Why?" Casey asked, wiping her eyes.

"I want to leave you the car so you and Lilly can come to the restaurant for lunch today," she answered, "after the rush is over. That okay with you?"

"Sure, Mom. Something special going on at the restaurant?"

"Maybe," her mom answered circuitously, "we'll have to see when you get there. Besides, today's special is chicken and dumplings."

Casey's eyebrows went up. All the better, she thought to herself. She loved chicken and dumplings. But, even the aniticpation of her favorite meal couldn't dissuade her from worrying about Mandy.

***

Mandy, it seemed, was on quite a few people's minds that morning. Not the least of whom was the Sheriff's. Down at the Sheriff Department's Headquarters, Sheriff Colter was on the phone with Mrs. Banks. He was seated in his office behind his desk and, from the look on his face, he was not pleased with the response he was getting.

"When was the last time you saw your daughter, Mrs. Banks?" he asked. He listened patiently and then explained, "Yes, I realize it's been painful for her. But, she's going to have to talk with me about it. I'll try to be as sensitive to her loss as I can, but you've got to keep in mind, a young boy was murdered." He listened again. "Yes, ma'am, but she may know more than she realizes." He paused, then said firmly, "Mrs. Banks, I expect you to call me as soon as she returns home. His demeanor softened, he was pleased to hear her reply. "Good...good, thank you, ma'am."

Colter hung up the phone, then walked out of his office and yelled to one of his deputies, "I'll be back in about two hours, gotta make a run up to the Delta Blues."

It was a little over an hour later, when Colter drove up the road that led to the Delta Blues Nightclub. He knew that anything and everything that happened within a hundred mile radius usually got filtered through King Luther's place, if only by word of mouth. Pulling into the parking lot of the Delta Blues in the harsh light of day was not unlike the sensation of flat beer and stale pretzels after an all night drunk. The sparkle and excitement of the original pleasure were long gone.

Jeff Colter parked his patrol car near the front entrance. He had come to talk about the murder. Exiting his vehicle, he squinted his eyes at the glare of the rising sun. It's heat felt more oppressive that morning from the sudden, unexpected rise in humidity.

Colter slammed the door of his patrol car just as the front door to the Delta Blues opened. Standing in the full width of the doorway, his body engulfing it from frame to frame, was King Luther.

The two men stared at each other as Colter made his way towards the entrance. As soon as the Sheriff was in range, Luther reached out his hand and greeted the younger man.

"Jeff," he said, amicably, "it's good to see you. No matter what brings you by."

Colter took the big man's hand and shook it as he gave him a friendly pat on the shoulder. "Thank you, Luther. I just wish it was under better circumstances."

"Well, now, come on in," said Luther as he led the Sheriff inside the club.

The big empty room appeared cavernous with its solitary stage and vacant tables and chairs. There was no hint of the glamour and excitement that had attracted large crowds for many an evening's entertainment. But then, the mystery and magic of the Delta Blues only emerged in the shadows of the night, long after the sun had gone down.

112

The two men sat at a table next to the bar. A large glass of prune juice was sitting on the table along with a tall glass of cold water. Luther took a swig of his prune juice and then placed the glass of water in front of Colter.

"Figured you'd be runnin' hot. You sure I can't get you something a little more substantial?"

"Water will do me just fine. Thanks."

"Always the purist...just like your dad was."

"Well, I sure as heck can't figure how you can drink that stuff. You ask me, it taste like old motor oil that's been sittin' out collecting dust somewhere."

"Just when you been sippin' old motor oil?" Luther laughed. "You ask me, you'd be a sight better off drinking a glass of prune juice." He took another swig. "Besides, it keeps me running like a clock."

Colter smirked, "Well, as long as it keeps you whistling 'Dixie.'"

Luther's eyebrows shot up. "Dixie!?" he said indignantly. He pretended to give Colter the evil eye. "Now, I know why my James turned out to be such a smart mouthed boy. Taggin' along with you on all them fishin' trips, learnin' all them smart mouthed ways."

Both men laughed.

"How is James?"

"So far, so good. They got him stuck somewhere over in southeast Asia. They're talkin' about sending him out to chase down some outfit they call the Viet Cong."

Colter could see the concern on Luther's face.

"James knows how to take care of himself, Luther. He's a smart kid."

A melancholy look swept over Luther's broad face. "Yeah, well, I hear things are startin' to heat up over there. I just pray they don't get too far outta hand."

"Next time you write him, tell him I said, 'hey.'"

Luther nodded, assuring that he would.

"Well, I know you're here on business. You said you got a picture you want me to take a look at."

Colter reached into his left shirt pocket and pulled out a school photo of a teenage boy. He handed it to Luther.

Luther took one quick look at it and began shaking his head.

"I knew that boy would come to no good."

"You know him?"

"I've seen him around. When you called, I figured it might be him. He's been here a couple of times. Dealin' dope, and I'm not talkin' maryjane. I warned him. I told him he was headed for trouble."

"Dope? Where the hell does a kid like that get his hand on hard drugs?"

Luther smirked. "We see it all here. Sometimes it's more than I can stomach. It's goin' mainstream, spreading like a disease through my people. I mean, I always kinda looked the other way when somebody did a reefer every now and again, but not with this stuff. This is hard core."

"Where's it coming from?"

"Not sure. Some sorry looking characters started showing up about six, seven months ago. Comin' in here ever so often, drinking and acting like they owned the place. You know the type. Real bad business."

"Got any idea who they are?"

"One of 'em, a scuzzy looking little guy, calls himself Weasel. Every now and again a big 'ol white boy, a great big bull of a guy, came in with him. Never caught his name."

"You ever see them with Eddie Burkette?"

"The boy in the picture?"

"Yeah."

"No."

"When did you first see the Burkette kid pushing dope?"

"About three months ago. We weren't sure what he was up to at first until one of my bouncers saw him dealin' in the parking lot. Last time he showed up he dealt his filth right over there, right from the bar. That's when we kicked his scrawny behind outta here."

"You got any idea where these creeps might be hanging out?"

114

"Not a clue. I'll put out some feelers if you want."

"I'd appreciate it. I got more than a bad feelin' about these jokers."

"I told that boy. I told him he was in over his head."

Colter gulped down the rest of his water and got up to leave.

"Better get."

"Don't be a stranger."

The two men looked at each other. There was a bond between them that had melded long ago. It was born out of the trust and friendship that existed between Colter's father and Luther when both were dirt poor and prejudice was as rampant as grit blowing in the wind on a gusty day. Colter knew that his father's and Luther's lives had crossed at an early age and their loyalty to one another was formed after a horrible incident. All Colter knew about the occurrence that had brought the two men together was that one of them had saved the other's life and that neither man would talk about it. Colter had always remained curious though, but respected both men enough to let the matter rest. Now with his dad gone, it would be up to Luther to reveal their secret, if he ever decided to do so. But, to that day, he had chosen to keep it to himself.

Colter nodded at Luther and headed for the door. After a few feet, he stopped suddenly and turned around and looked at him.

"You think it'd be okay if I drop James a line every now and again? You know, see how he's doin'?"

"I think he'd like that, Jeff. Fact, I think he'd like that a lot. Soon as I find out, I'll let you know where they're stationing him."

"Great. Take it easy, Luther."

11) LIFE'S SUDDEN INTRUSIONS

Several hours had passed and Camille had long been at work, when the old, beaten-up Chevy Impala made its way out of the neighborhood. The car was mostly dingy-gray with only specks of its former light blue paint still hanging on from its glory days. Nobody claimed it was much to look at, but compared to the old Hudson, it ran like a top. Getting where they needed to go was, after all, what mattered most to its two occupants.

Casey was at the wheel. Lilly was in the passenger's seat messing with the car radio. As Lilly twisted and turned the dial on the old radio, a mish-mash of various music squawked out.

Casey looked at her impatiently, "Lilly, you've gotta pick something," After a few more loud squawks and bleats from the radio, Lilly suddenly stopped on one song, "Blue Berry Hill," by Fats Domino.

Casey looked at her surprised, and said, "O-o-okay."

As Casey drove towards town, the music belted out of the radio. She glanced over Lilly. Enthralled with her selection, Lilly was happily tapping her little fingers on the car seat in rhythm with the music. Much to Lilly's delight, Casey smiled and then began to sing along. When Casey let rip a low, guttural, bluesy, "I found my thrill...on Blueberry Hill," Lilly grinned from ear-to-ear and let out a giggle. Casey grinned back, "All right, all right," she said, conceding to a beaming Lilly, "I'll admit it, you picked a pretty good song."

Lilly continued tapping her fingers to the music, enjoying the moment. Sometimes the sisters felt a certain closeness that nobody else could share.

As Casey sang along, she glanced in her rearview mirror. She noticed that a black Pontiac was following a short distance behind. Inexplicably, something deep in the recesses of her brain caused her body to tense slightly. Instinctively, she looked over at Lilly. Uncertain as to the cause of her uneasiness, she glanced in the rearview mirror again. The black car was still behind her. Not liking what she saw, she made a right turn. Once more, she glanced in the rearview mirror and watched as the black Pontiac also made a right turn and continued to follow behind her. A sudden sinking feeling overwhelmed her.

She gripped her fingers tightly around the steering wheel and sped up. She made a quick left turn heading towards town, looked in the mirror again and watched as the Pontiac also took a left. Determined to lose it, she quickly turned off the radio and picked up more speed. She passed a truck, then another car. Fearfully, she glanced in the rearview mirror again. The black Pontiac had disappeared. Relieved, she took several deep breaths. Then, one more time, to make absolutely certain, she cautiously looked in the rearview mirror a final time. Nothing was there. Still a little uneasy, she looked over at Lilly.

"Guess I've got a bad case of the jitters today."

Trying to shake off her anxiety, Casey reached over and clicked the radio back on. By this time, a ballad was playing. "There, that's better," she sighed to herself as she glanced at Lilly.

Minutes later, the girls pulled into town and up to Shey's Restaurant. Casey parked in front. She and Lilly got out. Casey looked around briefly. Seeing nothing out of the ordinary, she and Lilly went inside the restaurant.

Most of the center tables were already filled with the regular noon day crowd. Casey led Lilly over to an empty booth by the window. Seeing them, their mom smiled and waved to them. Casey waved back as she and Lilly scooted into the booth. After checking on some customers, Camille quickly made her way over to her daughters, carrying a couple of Cokes.

"Hi, girls," she greeted them cheerfully.

"Hi, Mom," said Casey.

Lilly happily looked up as her mom gave her kiss on the cheek, then took the Coke from her mother's hand and drank it down.

Camille continued, "You girls ready for some chicken and dumplings?"

Casey pretended dismay, "Mom...like you have to ask?"

"Good," Camille grinned, "'cause lunch will be out in a minute."

As Camille turned to go check on their order, she found herself face-to-face with Sheriff Jeff Colter. He had a look of concern on his face.

"Hope I'm not late," he said, apologetically.

They all looked up at him. He smiled. Camille smiled back, warmly.

"Jeff. Hi."

Hearing her mom call the Sheriff "Jeff" gave Casey a bit of a start.

"You're right on time," Camille told him.

Puzzled, Casey looked at them both. "For what?" she asked.

"Lunch," beamed her mother. "Sheriff Colter is joining us today."

He looked at the two girls, "How ya doin', Casey? Hi, Lilly." He turned towards Camille and said, "Camille, can I have a word with you?"

Hearing the Sheriff call her mom "Camille" gave Casey another start. She looked at them curiously as they moved a short distance away.

Standing near the office door, Sheriff Colter shifted awkwardly from foot to foot. Glancing around at the staring waitresses, he leaned over and whispered in Camille's ear.

"You sure you wouldn't prefer we all go somewhere a little more private?"

Camille shrugged her shoulders and smiled. "I gave it some thought. I figure since they're all going to find out about us sooner or later...sooner seemed as good a time as any."

"Ah-hah," he responded. "I get it. You figure we should hit 'em with the old *'undercut-the-gossip-and-face-em-head-on'* sort of strategy. Right?"

She giggled, "Something like that."

"Not bad, " he joked, "kinda throw them off their game."

Suddenly, "sooner" presented itself <u>sooner</u> than expected in the form of one of the aforementioned waitresses as she stepped between the two of them. She took a moment and first eyed Colter, sizing him up, before speaking to Camille.

"Camille, excuse me if I'm interrupting anything important, but Darla needs your help. She's having trouble with the register. She thinks it's stuck again."

Camille nodded at the waitress and shrugged her shoulders. She looked back at Colter, "Tell the girls, I'll be right there."

He smiled, "I will. Do what you've gotta do."

As Camille headed towards the counter, Colter went back over to the booth and sat down. He noticed Casey looking out of the window, staring intently at a black Pontiac as it drove slowly by the restaurant.

"Somebody you know?" he asked her. "Huh?" Casey said, distracted. Casey looked at him and then out the window again. "Uh, I'm not really sure," she said.

He waited for a second to see if she had further comment. Casey shrugged and looked at him. Not wanting to intrude, he let it slide.

"Your mom's gotta work out some problem with the cash register. She'll be over as soon as she's finished."

Casey looked at him curiously, "You here to talk about the case?"

"No," he replied, "it's something of a more personal nature."

She stared at him for a minute, then said casually, "You and Mom?"

"That obvious, uh?"

"Pretty much. Was she out with you last night?"

"She was," he nodded.

"Was it the first time?" she continued.

"Yep," he answered directly, "but it probably won't be the last."

Casey's eyes opened wide. "Is it serious?"

"Could be."

"*Could* be?" she said, as if questioning his intentions.

120

"Yeah," he replied. "The thing is...we just wanna make sure it's all right with you two first."

"Really?" said a surprised Casey.

"Really," he said, reassuringly.

Casey sat back in the booth. Attempting to digest what she had just heard, she again noticed the black Pontiac cruising by out in front of the restaurant. Colter noticed her wince, slightly. He looked out at the car.

"What's with the black Pontiac?" he asked.

"I think I know where I first saw it," she said as her memory began to jog.

"It was the last day of school. Eddie Burkette was talking to a bunch of guys. They were in a car kinda like that."

Colter's jaw tensed as he again looked out of the window. He looked back at Casey, then quickly slid out of the booth and headed for the door.

Outside on the sidewalk in front of Shey's restaurant, Colter looked to the left and then to the right for the Pontiac. It was nowhere in sight. He walked out into the middle of the street and again looked both directions. The car was nowhere to be seen. He glanced back at the restaurant window where he could clearly see Casey and Lilly sitting in the booth. Frustrated, he went back inside the restaurant.

Once back in the main dining area, Colter returned to the booth and sat down with Casey. She could see he was uneasy. His demeanor had taken on an air of seriousness.

"How many times have you seen that car?" he asked her.

"A few times," she told him. "I...I thought it was following me today...when we were on our way to the restaurant. But, I made some turns and it disappeared."

Hearing this, Colter's eyes took on a coldness Casey had not seen before. It was obvious to her that something was terribly wrong.

***

Later that evening at Casey's house, there was an unmistakable tension. The mood, at best, was extremely troublesome. Casey and Lilly were seated on the sofa in the living room while their mom sat in a chair. Sheriff Colter paced in front of them distracted by his own thoughts. He suddenly stopped and looked directly at Camille.

"I don't want to alarm you...I could be wrong...but they probably think that, somehow, Casey knows something about the murder," he concluded.

Camille was incredulous, "But, Jeff, it's so remote. I don't see how there can possibly be a connection."

"Camille -- Casey saw the Burkette boy getting shoved around by some guys in a black car. She's near the woods the day the he gets killed. Today, this same black car appeared to be following her. She saw it circle the restaurant a couple of times. I saw it myself," he insisted.

Camille was clearly distressed by his indisputable logic. A slight shiver crept up her spine as she realized how close Casey had been to danger. As much as she did not want to believe it, she knew she had to consider that what he was saying was true.

"Mom?" Casey interrupted.

"What, sweetheart?"

"I think it dropped Mandy off here at the house last night."

Camille was stunned, "What are you talking about?"

"The black car, " Casey explained, "I got a glimpse of it when it dropped Mandy off to spend the night."

"Oh my God!" exclaimed Camille.

"Are you sure?" asked Colter.

"Uh-huh, pretty sure," answered Casey, becoming more concerned as the events started coming together like some crazed puzzle.

Distraught, Camille looked at Colter, "Jeff, who are these people?"

"I don't know yet," he said, "but, I'm sure as hell gonna find out."

He looked at Casey, "Casey, if you see that car again, you call me. Don't try to do anything, just call me right away."

Casey nodded just as the phone rang. She got up to answer it. With Casey out of the room, a frightened Camille looked up at Colter, "What possible connection could there be between all this and that murder?" she asked.

"Someone may think that Casey saw what happened in the woods that day."

Camille's face turned ashen. "And what...now they're coming after her?"

"I don't know. Until I do," he insisted, "she's going to have to take precautions."

"Precautions?" There was panic in Camille's voice. "Jeff, they drove up to our house! Mandy is supposed to be Casey's friend, for God's sake."

"That's just it. They may be using the Banks girl to get to Casey."

"If that's true, then Mandy could be in danger as well. This is really frightening, Jeff. We've got to do something."

He tried to reassure her, "Camille, I'll talk with the Bank's girl first thing tomorrow. She may be in deeper than she realizes." He paused for a second and then said as calmly as he could, "I think it will be best if you keep the girls close to home for the time being."

Camille nervously nodded in agreement.

***

In the hallway, Casey held the phone to her ear, listened patiently and then once more insisted, "No, Mrs. Banks, like I said, Mandy's not here." She listened again, then: "No ma'am, I'm sorry. I haven't seen her since this morning. But, if I do hear from her, I'll be sure to tell her you are looking for her."

***

The likelihood of anyone finding Mandy's whereabouts was slim to none. Even in small towns, there are some places that are out-of-sight, out-of-mind and long forgotten. Cutahey's was one of them. But then, that had been the initial plan all along.

Cutahey's Lounge was originally set back -- from the main highway -- out of sight, so as to go undetected by any curious passers-by. Strategically positioned atop a small hill, it served well as an observation post. Anyone staring out of its windows could easily catch sight of approaching lawmen.

Gambling and booze had long been its main attraction before old man Cutahey's sudden demise one night in the middle of a poker game. But, even many years later, as it sat there weathered and decaying -- a boarded up shell of its former self -- it still managed to attract unsavory characters.

It was mid-afternoon and the mood was disgruntled, to say the least, as music could be heard coming out of the old lounge. The black Pontiac was parked out in front with its rear end pointed downward on the graveled parking lot. Bull and Weasel -- Mole's two thugs -- were sitting on the front porch. Bull was in an irritable frame of mind.

"I'm gettin' sick and tired of this, " he grumbled. "What the hell we gotta wait out here for?"

Weasel looked over at him, "Relax, Bull. Mole don't want no distractions."

Bull's foul mood turned darker, "'Mole don't want no distractions...Mole don't want no distractions.' Is that all you can say? No wonder he calls you Weasel."

"Shsss...shsss," Weasel cautioned as he looked back over his shoulder hoping they had not been overheard by Mole. "Look, man," said Weasel, lowering his voice, "he don't want that chick catching sight of us. He's afraid if she sobers up, somethin' will click and she'll figure out we ain't exactly old friends of her dead boyfriend. Once he finds out what she knows about where the stuff is, it ain't gonna matter. Until then, I suggest you keep your trap shut and cool it."

Bull was too testy to go along -- to get along. "Don't tell me to cool it! You know as well as I do that this caper ain't going down right. First, Burkette takes a dive on us, now Mole's in there makin' sweet on his girl, we're chasin' some kid around...while he's damn near got us damn near livin' outta that damn car...and we still ain't got the stuff. Now, you know that ain't right!"

"Hey, man, I don't know nothin'. But, if I was you, I'd keep a lid on it. I'm just tellin' you this for your own good, Bull."

"And, quit callin' me Bull! I'm sick of using these freakin' names."

"It's our cover, man. Mole says it'll make it harder if somebody tries to track us. You know that."

Bull scowled, "Yeah, well, I don't give a big fat rat's behind. I think it's stupid. I always thought it was stupid."

"Yeah? Well, you tell him," said Weasel. "As for me, I'm just gonna sit here and mind my own business."

***

Inside Cutahey's, Mole had again busied himself behind the counter as Mandy laid stretched out on the old sofa. Once more having succumbed to her newly found comfort zone, she was downing another beer hoping to erase her pain in an endless stupor. As she laid back against the cushions, she held her beer out in front of her, the full length of her arm, and stared at it whimsically.

Watching her from behind the counter, Mole smirked, "You know, you ain't had one of them things out of your hands since I met you." He snickered to himself, "Unless your were sleepin'."

Mandy took another swig of her beer. "It helps me forget," she said, feebly. "It helps make the pain to go away." Mandy knew she was going down the wrong track, but had neither the desire nor sense to get off.

Mandy looked up at Mole and flinched. Once again, he had the hypodermic needle in his hand. Even in her inebriated state, she knew this was something she did not want. She recoiled back into the sofa.

"You want to ease the pain, babydoll?" he said as he reached down for her arm. "Mole's got just the thing that'll do it for you."

Mandy resisted, "No...I don't want it. I got sick."

"That was just the first time. I gave you too much. This time, you're gonna like it."

"Don't," she pleaded, her speech slurring. "I've heard about this stuff. They say...it's not good for you."

"Who said?"

"I don't know. People, you know?"

"People?" he chided her. "Who? A bunch of Dudley-do-rights who wouldn't know a good time if it sat on their faces?" He laughed. "Don't you know, they're just out to spoil it for the rest of us. This is prime stuff, baby. Anybody says otherwise, is a loser."

"I'm...I'm not a loser," Mandy insisted as Mole took her arm and tied it off. He injected the narcotic into her veins and she began to babble, "Eddie said, this town was for losers. He called it Losersville. We were getting out."

"I know, baby, you were gonna leave. Where were you and Eddie going?"

She started to cry, "I don't know. He said he was gonna take care of me."

"Hey, hey," he said hoping to gain her confidence, "don't you worry your little puddin' head about it. 'Ol Mole here will take care of you...just like Eddie woulda wanted."

"Whataya mean Eddie woulda wanted?" she asked, barely understanding anything he was saying.

"I already told ya...Eddie was a friend. He told me how much he loved you. Said, if anything happened to him, I should look after you. He trusted me."

"He did?"

"Yeah. See, baby, that's what it's all about...trust." He gave her as sincere a look as he could manage, "I been good to you so far, haven't I?"

Mandy stared at him as the drug started to pulse through her veins, "But, Eddie..."

Mole interrupted, "But, Eddie nothing, sweetheart. There ain't nothin' Eddie can do for you now."

Suddenly, the phone rang behind the bar. Mole patted her on the face, then went to answer it.

Mole picked up the receiver, "Yeah?"

He listened a moment, standing perfectly still. His eyes darted about in a crazed fashion as he listened intently to what was being said on the other end of the line. He then began to shift about nervously. As he leaned over the bar to steady himself, a bead of sweat broke out over his brow.

"J.C., I'm workin' on it," he said anxiously. "Look, calm down, man, I'm doing everything I can." He wiped the sweat away, becoming more agitated as he again listened.

"J.C...no, man," he said defensively, "it's not a problem. You don't have to do that." Mole flinched at the response. He then said, conceding, "Yeah...yeah, J.C....I'll be here."

He jerked his head away from the phone when the receiver on the other end was slammed down hard. His face twisted into an expression of fear and anger as he slammed down his own receiver and headed for the door. He opened it and screamed with a fury at Bull and Weasel.

"Get her! I don't care how you do it...just get her!"

Bull and Weasel scrambled off the porch, made a mad dash for the black Pontiac and hopped in. As they drove away, Mole angrily looked back inside the lounge at Mandy.

She turned and looked at him, groggily. "Who's J.C.?"

"Somebody you don't wanna know," he groused.

He went over to the sofa and pulled her head back by her hair.

"Time's running out, sweetheart. You and me, we gotta talk."

***

The following day, at the Castle's house, it was a far more idealistic scene as Camille, Casey and Lilly were all crowded into the kitchen. Camille had just finished washing Lilly's hair in the kitchen sink. As her mother rinsed the sink, Casey helped Lilly down from the chair and started to dry her hair with a large

127

towel. When the phone rang, Casey handed the towel off to her mom, who stooped down and continued to dry Lilly's wet, little head without missing a beat. Casey then headed for the hall way. She picked up the phone and said, "Hello."

She was delighted to hear the voice on the other end, "Oh, hi, Chance."

Next door at Mrs. Eberworth's house, Chance was in his grandmother's den on the phone. He was trying very hard not to be nervous, preferring to stand rather than sit comfortably on his grandmother's dark burgundy corduroy covered couch. As casually as he could, he uttered the opening line of his pre-planned and well-rehearsed conversation.

"Hey, how's it going?"

He listened to the response and smiled, relieved by the reception on the other end of the phone. "Yeah, me too. I've just been sorta...hanging around." Having managed to calm down somewhat, he fired off question number two, "Nice day, isn't it?" Hearing yet another receptive response, he became a bit more assured. "Yeah, could be a hot one," he agreed, "I heard it could get as high as 90 degrees....maybe hotter."

With his initial jitters finally fading and having survived the requisite small talk, he figured it was time to get down to business. Mustering his courage, he was ready to unload his final question.

"Look, I get off work early tomorrow," he said. Suddenly...WHAM!! He was hit like a bolt of lightning. No sooner than he had begun, his mouth went as dry as the desert sand and he could hear his heart rapidly pounding in his ear like a bass drum. Flustered by the sudden onslaught of bad nerves, he broke into a cold sweat. But, it was too late to turn back. All he could do was plow forward.

"I...I was wondering if you'd like to catch a movie or something? I hear they're showing a new James Bond flick. It's supposed to be really good. I mean if you'd like to go, I was thinking it'd probably be a good movie. you know, to go see. I mean, together...you and me." Dazed, he took a deep breath.

Then, an odd thing happened. It was like something had drifted between the houses, through the air. Casey, it seemed, had also become afflicted. She wondered to herself if it could be the heat as her knees began to feel like warm caramel left out too long in the noon day sun. With all of her discernible thought processes starting to shut down, her legs threatened to give way at any second. She struggled as best she could to maintain her composure.

She had heard the question -- she was certain she did. Otherwise, why would she be experiencing sudden brain-lock. With her mind barely functional, a voice inside was struggling to get her attention. It was telling her that she had to say something now or she would come off looking like a first-class dim-wit. The latter, by far, being the worse of the two, she enthusiastically blurted out:

"James Bond. I'd love it. I hear it's really great. I can't believe we're really going to go see it! I mean," she said, trying to calm down, "I'm really glad you thought about me. Hold on a minute, okay. I gotta check with my mom. You know, make sure it's all right"

Well, there...she had managed to say something. Nothing that she could instantly recall. But, at the moment, it really didn't matter. Clasping her hand over the receiver, she yelled out, "Mom! Mom! Is it okay if I go to the movies tomorrow?"

Camille entered the hallway with a tousled haired Lilly in tow.

"Casey, I don't see how that's possible. I'm working," she explained.

"Mom..." moaned an exasperated Casey.

"You know good and well, young lady, that I need you to stay here and take care of Lilly."

Still holding the phone in her hands, Casey looked over at Lilly as if she had suddenly become the enemy.

"Mom, I always have to take care of Lilly," she lamented. "Can't you take the day off or something?"

Camille dismissed her daughter's foolish suggestion without further consideration.

"Yeah, right, like I'm going to miss a day's pay so you can go to the movies. For God's sake, Casey, grow up."

Casey looked at her mother as if her world had ended.

Camille was completely unaffected by it, "Don't...give me that hang-dog look. It's not going to work this time."

Casey was way beyond hang-dog.

"Besides," her mother continued, "as long as that black car is prowling around, I don't want you leaving this house. You understand?"

"Yes, ma'am."

Camille continued on her way to the bedroom with Lilly.

Frustrated, Casey sighed into the phone, "I can't go. My mom needs for me to look after Lilly." She fiddled with the phone cord, wrapping it around her finger as she continued, "But...thanks for asking. Maybe some other time, okay?"

Feeling trapped and upset, she hung up the phone. Her disappointment was unmistakable as her face appeared to have settled into a permanent droop.

***

The next day turned out to be another beautiful summer's day. Camille had long since left for work. Despite the sunny clouds outdoors, storm clouds were unmistakably brewing inside. The two girls were in the living room. Lilly stubbornly stood by the front door. She wanted to go out. Casey was tugging at her little sister by the arm, attempting to pull her away from the door.

"Lilly, we are not going out! You may as well forget it. Mama said, we have to stay inside."

Lilly was not budging. She reached for the knob. Casey again pulled her hand away. Lilly stubbornly yanked her hand free from Casey's grasp and gripped the door knob again.

"That's it!" yelled Casey. "I think it's time for you to take a nap, young lady."

Lilly stood there defiantly. She was not going anywhere but out.

"Oh, so that's the way it's going to be!?" Casey could recognize a stand-off when she saw one. "Well, we'll see about that!" she said.

Casey grabbed Lilly's arm and tried to pull her away from the door. Lilly held tight. Suddenly, they were in a real tug-of-war. As the two girls scuffled about, Casey suddenly lost her grip on Lilly and fell backwards, whacking her head on the wooden arm of the rocking chair as she tumbled downward. She howled out in pain, lying on the floor, holding her head.

"Damn it, Lilly!"

Casey got up and angrily grabbed Lilly and whacked her on the side of the leg. Determined, Lilly bolted towards the door again. Casey lost her cool.

"I have just about had it!! Do you hear me!?" Casey reached out and grabbed Lilly by the arm, yanked her away from the door and sent her younger sister flying across the room. Losing her balance, Lilly tumbled down onto the floor.

Stunned and with her feelings sorely hurt, Lilly stared up in dismay. Her lip started to quiver. Huge tears welled up in her eyes. As she looked up at her older sister, a very pained look crossed her face. Without so much as making a sound, she started to cry as if her very heart was broken. Casey watched as the silent tears rolled down her face. Shocked by her own actions and crushed at the sight of Lilly's tears, Casey was devastated.

"Oh my God, Lilly." Oh, my God, I'm so sorry. I...I didn't mean to do that. You know I'd never hurt you. Oh God, I'm so sorry." Tears began streaming down her own face. She tried to explain as she went over, reached down and gently helped Lilly to her feet.

"Everything is just so messed up right now," she said, straightening Lilly's shirt which had gotten slightly twisted about during their tussle. "I didn't mean to take it out on you. It's not your fault."

She led the still distraught Lilly over to the rocking chair and sat her down.

Lilly was too hurt to look at her. Casey took her sister's small hands in hers and held them as she spoke softly to Lilly.

"Sweetie, I would love to take you walking. But, we can't leave the house. I wish...I just wish I could make you understand."

Casey gently wiped the tears from her little sister's face. "Would you like a Coke? We can watch TV."

Hearing the word "Coke," Lilly perked up a little and looked at her sister. Casey looked into her sweet, little innocent face. She softly kissed her on the cheek.

"Baby, I didn't mean to hurt you. I promise I won't ever do it again. Okay? What do you say we just stay in and drink Cokes till we float...okay?"

Casey headed for the kitchen and got a couple of Cokes. As she returned and was handing one to a more contented Lilly, there was a knock at the door. Casey looked through the blinds. She wiped away the last of her own tears and opened the door. Chance stood on the front porch, feeling slightly awkward, uncertain of his reception.

"I got off early today," he said. "Thought I'd come by. It was like...just a walk across the yard, you know."

A hint of a smile crossed Casey's face, "Yeah...I know."

Casey looked down and saw that Chance had brought his grandmother's dog, Sport, with him.

"Hey, Sport."

"He's just had a bath. I told him he couldn't come over unless he got himself cleaned up."

Casey smiled. She could see Chance had made some effort himself. Every hair was in place and he was obviously freshly scrubbed. His creme-colored khaki pants had a fine-line crease in them and his light blue pull-over accentuated his summer tan.

"You both look pretty sharp, if you ask me."

"Yeah?"

"Yeah."

Casey could see a hint of rose come into his cheeks as he blushed slightly. She quickly reached down and patted the Labrador Retriever on its head. As she did so, Chance pulled a bag from behind his back and handed it to her. "Thought you guys might like these."

Surprised, she gave him a huge grin as she took the bag. She opened it and looked in. "Chocolate chip cookies," she practically swooned as if they were diamonds, "Lilly will love them."

Beaming, she looked at him, "You...you wanna come in?"

Without hesitation, Chance went into the house, leaving Sport on the porch. Lilly looked up from her Coke as he entered.

"Hi, Lilly," he said.

Casey took the cookies out of the bag, "Look, Lilly. Look what Chance brought us." Casey opened the cookies and gave Lilly a couple. As far as Lilly was concerned, all was forgiven.

Casey then took one cookie for herself and one for Chance. As she handed it to him, he looked at her closely.

"Are you all right?" he asked noticing her slightly reddened eyes.

"Why?"

"Eyes seem kinda puffy."

"Oh. It was...uh. Lilly and I had a little misunderstanding."

He was surprised, "You and Lilly?"

"Yeah. You might say she straightened me out on a few things. She wants to go for a walk. We can't. I overreacted."

"So, why not meet her half way? We can sit on the porch. She can play with Sport. Might not be a walk, but at least she's outside."

Casey thought about his suggestion for a second. Sounded reasonable to her. She brightened up, "Sure. Why not? Works for me."

"Great," he said, "everybody might not get exactly what they want...but it's a pretty fair settlement." He looked over at Lilly as she took another bite out of her cookie, "What do you think, you up for it, Lilly?

Casey eyed him suspiciously. "Wait a minute," she said curiously, "what's going on here? What'd she do? Get her lawyer over here to plead her case?"

Chance flashed one of his charming grins. He gave her a shrug... admitting to nothing.

"Okay, fine," said Casey, acting like she was giving in. "Let me check with your client. See if she's up for the compromise." They both looked over at Lilly and couldn't help but chuckle as she sat there complacently enjoying her cookies and Coke.

Being in the wrong place at the wrong time can be a tough turn of luck. A person's fate becomes evident fairly quickly for anyone caught in such unfortunate circumstances.

Back at Cutahey's, the situation had far from improved for Mandy. She had become the full focus of Mole's attention and for anyone, especially Mandy, that was not a good place to be. As she sat timidly on a bar stool, Mole was emptying the contents of her purse onto the counter. Strewn about among a handful of wadded up Kleenex were a lipstick, comb, compact powder case, a wallet-sized picture of Eddie and a few dollars and some change. Mole rummaged through her belongings, pushing aside several of the items. Suddenly, his eyes narrowed. Sitting there among the clutter, looking oddly out of place, was a small key.

He looked at Mandy, delighted with his discovery, "What's this we got here?"

He held the small key up in front of Mandy, eyeing her suspiciously, "Eddie give you this?"

Hesitating, Mandy looked at Mole, then at the key.

As Mole leaned forward, pressing her for an answer, she could feel his breath on her face.

"Did Eddie give you this key?"

She quickly answered him. "No, no, it's a house key," she insisted.

Mole held the key between his fingers, examining it...as if it were the key to all of his problems.

"Sweetheart, this ain't no house key. Now it may be a post office box key, or a bus station locker key or some other kind of key...but, this ain't no house key."

He cocked his head to the side and looked at her, "You trying to hide something from 'ol Mole?"

"I don't know what you're talking about," she stammered.

"Then let me spell it out it for you," he said coolly. He wrapped her hair in his fist and pulled her towards him.

"Here's the thing," he told her. "Eddie had something that belonged to me. And, like any good friend, he wanted to make sure I got it back. I figure, maybe he mentioned it to you. Told you where he was keeping it."

He got right in her face, "Maybe even asked you to keep it safe for me."

Mandy didn't budge. She continued to stonewall him.

"Eddie never said nothin'. In fact, I don't even recall him ever mentioning your name."

Growing increasingly impatient, Mole gripped her hair tightly in his hand.

Wincing at the pain, she reached up and tried to pull his hand away. He tightened his grip, yanked her off of her bar stool and, in a fit of anger, picked it up and sent it crashing across the floor. Mandy looked at him, startled. A violent look in his eye told her she was on the brink of some very serious trouble.

Mandy watched nervously as he struggled to get control of himself. He meticulously placed the small key back on the counter top and then looked at her as he explained matter-of-factly.

"You picked a bad time to give me grief. I got a problem that's gonna come through that door in about four hours. His name is J.C. and he ain't gonna be allowing no negotiations in my behalf. Last time he set foot in this place, he killed a man, shot him dead out. It was 'ol man Cutahey himself. J.C. accused him of cheatin' him at cards. So, for starters, he ain't gonna be too keen on coming here and scaring up old ghosts." Mole got right in her face, "What I'm tellin you...is my neck is on the line. So, you and me, sweetheart...are through dancin' around."

He suddenly *slapped* her hard, knocking her off her feet and onto the floor. Mandy cowered in fear.

"Now," said Mole, "let's start again. You tell me what you know about this key."

***

As dismal and threatening as Mandy's world had become, things could not have been brighter or more carefree back at Casey's house. Enjoying the warmth of the afternoon sun, Casey and Chance watched from the porch as Lilly frolicked with Sport on the grass.

Lilly giggled with glee as the dog bounced around her, then knocked her backwards off of her feet to the ground. Seeing Lilly fall to the ground, Casey and Chance became alarmed. But, Lilly quickly sprang back into action. Sport continued to bounce around her, playfully lunging at her and nuzzling his head in her chest. Laughing even harder as the game progressed, Lilly took a swing at Sport, smacking him flat on the nose with her opened palm, causing him to yelp loudly. He then let out a low growl. Hearing the dog's bark turn to a growl, Chance and Casey immediately got to their feet. But, before they knew it, Sport was back in the game, frolicking again with Lilly as if nothing had happened.

Chance was intrigued that Sport was so willing to take the abuse. He watched curiously how the dog responded so naturally to Lilly.

Without editing his thoughts, he spoke candidly to Casey, "It's amazing, isn't it, how animals are so gentle with kids like Lilly. You know, who are..."

He stopped, embarrassed. Casey looked at Lilly and then back at Chance.

"Retarded?" She said it openly.

"Yeah," he said, feeling her ease with the subject. "It's like they've got a sense about it. Like they can tell."

As if on cue, Sport playfully charged at Lilly again. Lilly let out a loud squeal as she pushed him away. Casey and Chance laughed as they watched the two of them play.

Completely immersed in what had turned out to be a surprisingly engaging afternoon together, neither Casey nor Chance noticed the black Pontiac that was parked down the street a block away. They were unaware as the car's engine quietly rumbled to a start. At that moment, sitting there on the front porch, Casey and Chance were not mindful of anything outside of themselves and Lilly and Sport. Their conversation took a more personal turn as the black car started to slowly move up the block towards the house.

"I'm glad you came over," said Casey unabashedly. "Hope you're not too bummed about missing the movie."

"No big thing", said Chance. "Besides, who needs James Bond? Just a lot of action...intrigue...and fast cars. Right?"

"Right," she agreed. "Who needs all that international mayhem when we can sit on my front porch and watch Lilly beat up Sport."

The best Casey was able to manage was a half-hearted laugh at her own joke. She was still feeling somewhat deprived about missing their movie date. Feeling equally ambivalent, Chance offered a solution, "Maybe, I can schedule some time off when your mom doesn't have to work..."

Before he finished his sentence, Casey was distracted by something moving up the street. She glanced up as the black Pontiac slowly approached the house. She gasped.

Chance looked at her. "What is it?" he asked as he followed her gaze.

"That black car. We've got to get inside."

"Why?" he wanted to know. "What about it?"

"They've been following me. I don't know why. But, I'm not going to sit here and find out."

As the car started to pick up speed, Casey leapt from the porch and ran towards Lilly. She grabbed her hand and pulled her up off of the grass. The black car lurched to the curb. Chance was there to meet it. He hesitated momentarily, but held his position as Bull's massive frame came barreling out of the passenger's side straight at him. Clearly, Bull was twice the size of the teenager, but Chance had little choice but to meet him head-on. The two slammed into one another. Chance suddenly found himself being lifted off his feet, high into the air. Chance quickly wrapped one arm around Bull's huge neck, squeezed it tightly and hung on for dear life.

Wasting no time, Weasel had jumped out of the driver's side of the car and was headed straight for the girls. Casey was hurrying Lilly up the front steps into the house when Weasel grabbed her arm and pulled her back down onto the sidewalk. Not about to give up without a fight, Casey took a swing at her attacker. Weasel ducked low to avoid taking the hit, only to meet up with Casey's right knee and what felt like a tooth-shattering blow underneath his chin.

Bull, meanwhile, had managed to pry Chance's arm loose from around his neck. Then, virtually manhandling the teenager, he swung him around, threw him off of his huge body and onto the ground. By then, Weasel had gotten the upper hand in his struggle with Casey. Within seconds, he too was flinging her across the yard onto the ground. Before Casey was able to regain her footing, Weasel lunged at Lilly, grabbed her off her feet and ran with her towards the car.

Weasel tossed Lilly into the front seat just as Sport sank his teeth into Weasel's pant leg and began tugging on it, growling ferociously. Back on her feet, Casey was making a valiant run towards the car to save her little sister.

"Noooo!" she screamed, "let her go!"

Her effort proved fruitless as Bull blocked her path. He grabbed her with one hand and easily tossed her, like a feather, onto the sidewalk.

Seeing Lilly in the Pontiac, Chance lunged at Weasel and pulled him away from the car. As Chance wrestled with Weasel, Bull came up from behind, spun Chance around and flattened him with a blow across the jaw. Bull then looked down at Sport who was growling with his fangs still firmly clamped onto Weasel's pants. In one swift motion, Bull drew back his leg and kicked Sport hard in the ribs sending him flying into the yard, yelping in pain.

Having watched the entire skirmish with some interest, Lilly sat in the black Pontiac and looked on calmly as the two thugs hurriedly piled into the car beside her. The car pulled away from the curb, tires squealing, as Casey ran after it desperately screaming.

"Lilly!! Lilly!! Somebody stop them! Please...stop them!"

***

No one over at Shey's Restaurant could possibly be aware of the situation back at Casey's house. By contrast, activities at the restaurant could only be described as routine. It was just another busy day as Sheriff Colter came through the front door. One of the waitresses noticed him, smiled knowingly and motioned him towards the back office. He nodded at her and headed for the office door.

Camille was on the phone in the restaurant's back office. She impatiently held the receiver to her ear as it rang...and rang...and rang.

The door to the office opened and Colter entered. He could see Camille's worried look.

"What's wrong?" he asked, concerned.

"Casey's not answering the phone. I told her. I told her not to go out." She listened for a few seconds longer, then said anxiously, "Jeff, I've got to get home."

"I'll take you," he volunteered.

Just as she was about to hang up, she heard a voice on the other end of the line. Relieved, she put the receiver back to her ear and spoke into the phone.

"Casey, for heaven's sake! What is going on? What took you so long to answer...?"

As Camille listened, her face became a mixture of emotions, "Wait a minute, honey, calm down. What are you saying...what about Lilly?"

She listened, astonished at what she was hearing, "Where is she now...?"

Colter could see the fear in her eyes. He moved protectively towards her.

Horrified, she screamed into the phone, "Oh, my God, no...please no. Not Lilly!"

***

Back at Cutahey's Lounge, the stakes had increased dramatically. Mole now had, not one, but two hostages on his hands. The newest, of which, had become the center of his attention.

Mandy was out cold on the couch, her face badly bruised. The latest addition to Mole's equation sat calmly in a chair that had been placed in front of the bar.

Mole sat on a bar stool -- staring at Lilly.

"Kid's one cool cucumber, ain't she? Nothin' seems to shake her," he said, intrigued by her calm demeanor.

"I'm tellin' ya, Mole," said Weasel, "there's something funny about this kid. She ain't said a word since we nabbed her."

"Too bad for her it's gonna be a permanent condition." He looked at her and smirked, "Can't have you tellin' tales on 'ol Mole and the boys, now can we, little darlin'?"

Bull anxiously looked at Mole, "Mole, she's just a kid."

Bull's comment had little effect other than to elicit a cold sneer. "What'd you think, fat head, you think you were bringing her here for a tea party?"

Bull looked, nervously, over at Weasel. Equally baffled as to what to do, Weasel could only shrug his shoulders. But, Bull wasn't backing off.

"I ain't doing no kid," he said emphatically.

Before he could continue, they were all interrupted by a small groan. It was Mandy. She was beginning to stir. She sat up and rubbed her swollen face.

Seeing her bruises, Weasel asked, "What happened to her?"

"A minor miscommunication," Mole responded sarcastically. "Girlfriend here finally decided she had a few things to tell me, once she got over her shyness, ain't that right, sugar?"

Mandy glared at him through her swollen eye, "You rotten pig, you lied to me. You're no friend of Eddie's."

"You got it all wrong, sweetheart. I was probably the best friend Eddie ever had. I'm the one guy Eddie could count on to be with him right to the very end." Mole laughed at the irony of his own statement.

"I've had enough of your crap," declared Mandy, "I'm gettin' outta here."

Mandy started to get up, but Mole snickered and pushed her back down on the sofa, "Like hell you are."

Bull stepped between her and the door to block her path should she attempt to make a run for it. Mandy looked around the room, sizing up her situation, then suddenly noticed Lilly.

Surprised, she asked, "Wha...what's she doing here?"

"You know her?" asked Mole. His eyes narrowed into small slits as he focused intently on Mandy. Mandy didn't answer. She sat there, perplexed -- staring at Lilly. Her mind raced, trying to make sense of Lilly's presence. The gruff sound of Mole's voice shook her back to reality.

"I asked you...do you know her?"

"Uh...no," she said, as she sank back into the sofa out of harm's way.

"Then don't ask questions," he sneered.

He then looked back over at Lilly.

"Like I was sayin', too bad for you, little girl, you had to be in the wrong place at the wrong time."

Mole slid down off his bar stool to go over to Lilly. As he approached her, he stopped cold, his body tensing up. Virtually frozen in place, a small panic rushed through him as he listened intently to the sounds of a car pulling up out front on to the graveled parking lot. Alarmed, he looked at the door.

"He's here," he said, turning a pale shade of gray as the blood rushed from his face.

He whirled around and looked anxiously at Bull and Weasel, "Nobody say nothin', you hear me? I'll do the talkin'." Then, glaring at Mandy, "And, you...you keep your mouth shut."

Mole's heart jumped as the front door suddenly swung open. Two bodyguards walked through it and proceeded into the lounge. They checked the premises without saying a word to anyone. As they did so, a third man entered. He did not appear to be in a sociable mood. He wore dark lensed glasses and was sporting closely cropped hair and a beard with sprinkles of gray.

His face was like granite. He cold eyes swept the room, stopping on Mole, who did his best not to appear nervous.

With a false bravado, Mole extended his greeting, "J.C., good to see ya, man."

J.C. did not respond. He looked at Lilly and then at Mandy.

"What are they doing here?" he demanded.

Mole shrugged his shoulders slightly. "Minor complications," he said, trying to make light of the situation. "Nothin' we can't take care of." Mole nervously started towards the bar. "Look, I'll explain everything, man." Whataya say we have a drink first and I'll lay it out for you."

"I asked you a question."

The icy cold reply stopped Mole in his tracks. J.C. was not someone he wanted to mess with. Without further delay, Mole pointed at Mandy and quickly explained, "This one's the punk's girlfriend. And, the kid...the kid was in the woods, watchin'...when we did Burkette."

Mole's admission slammed into Mandy's consciousness like a brick. Her mind was jarred by an avalanche of emotions. Unable to restrain herself, she flew off of the couch screaming and began pounding her fists on Mole's chest. "You murdering bastard! You killed him. You killed Eddie!"

Mole wrestled with her as Bull and Weasel dragged her off of him.

"I told you to shut-up!" he screamed.

Bull and Weasel tossed Mandy aside. She fell to the floor next to the bar.

J.C. watched the scene, his face cold and expressionless.

143

He then looked curiously over at Lilly who sat there watching the whole fracas, seemingly unmoved. J.C. noticed her apparent disinterest.

He looked directly at her and asked, "So, whatta you gotta say, kid?"

Lilly nonchalantly looked around the room. J.C. went over to her and leaned down menacingly in her face. "What's the matter, you deaf?"

"Leave her alone!" yelled Mandy.

J.C. glared at her, "This ain't any of your business."

Mandy got up from the floor and stood next to the bar.

"She doesn't talk," she said, tentatively, coming to Lilly's defense.

J.C.'s eyes narrowed, "What do you mean...she doesn't talk?"

"She never has," Mandy explained, "not since she was born."

J.C. gave Mandy a look that sent a chill down her spine, "What the hell are you tryin' to pull?"

"Nothing. It's true. I know her big sister, Casey...she's a friend of mine!"

J.C. looked at Mandy, curiously. Then stared, as if fixated, on Lilly for a moment.

"What's her name?"

"Lilly," answered Mandy.

J.C. stooped down beside Lilly and gently cupped her innocent face in his hand. Then with the quickness of a rattlesnake, he turned his wrath on Mole. He took one step towards him and cracked him hard across the jaw. Mole staggered backwards and J.C.'s two body guard's grabbed him from both sides. Bull and Weasel stood frozen in their spots.

J.C. looked at Lilly, then back at Mole and then bellowed, "What the hell do you think you're doing?!"

"J.C., she was a witness!" Mole clamored in his own defense.

"She's a kid! She doesn't even talk," he screamed. "You know what kind of heat this is? And for what?!"

Mole cringed as J.C. stepped towards him.

"You got a real disaster going here! You freakin' idiot."

The men continued to argue loudly. Mandy realized their momentary distraction provided her only chance. With great care, she slowly slipped down, unnoticed, behind the bar. As she did so, she slid the phone down with her.

Her heart pounding, she sat on the floor with the phone in her lap. Holding her breath, she began to dial. She was terrified of being discovered as the old rotary phone made a clackety-clack sound during each rotation.

Carefully, she dialed the five-digit number to Casey's house. Her hand shook as she held the receiver to her ear.

Anxiously waiting for someone to answer, she hovered over the phone, shielding the mouth piece with her hand. As the argument between the two men continued to heat up, a chair suddenly came flying over the bar's counter, smashing hard into the back wall. Mandy closed her eyes and cringed as it crashed loudly to the floor next to her. Opening her eyes, she looked at the chair, took a deep breath and again listened to the continuous ringing on the other end of the line.

Finally, she heard a voice answer. Carefully cupping her hand around the receiver, she whispered, "Casey. Casey...it's me. I'm at the old Cutahey's. They've got Lilly."

Mandy was startled by another loud crash. Frightened, she quickly hung up the phone. Placing it on the floor, she slowly got up from behind the counter. She saw Mole sprawled out on the floor. She watched as the two bodyguards yanked him to his feet, holding him as J.C. cracked him hard again across the jaw.

Blood spurted out of Mole's mouth. Mandy flinched and looked away. As she did so, she looked down at the counter and saw *the key*. It was just sitting there, on the bar, where Mole had left it.

She watched as J.C. hit Mole again, this time in the solar plexus. When Mole doubled over, she ever so carefully slid her hand over the small key and nestled it securely into the palm of her left hand.

***

Back at Casey's house, Mandy's phone call had brought both hope and desperation. The mood had become increasingly intense. Casey and Chance looked on anxiously as Camille spoke frantically into the phone,

"Please, you must get a message to Sheriff Jeff Colter. He just left here," she explained to the dispatcher on the other end of the line. "You have to tell him we've heard from Mandy."

Camille listened, intently. She again conveyed the message, "That's right, Mandy. All she said was that she and Lilly are being held at the old Cutahey's." Camille's voice became more urgent as she pleaded into the phone, "Please... please tell him to hurry. Please don't let them hurt my baby."

Casey went to her mother when she hung up the phone. They held tightly to each other for a moment. Then, staunchly pulling herself together, Camille looked at Casey and Chance.

"I want both of you...to stay here," she ordered.

Casey looked at her mother, confused. "Mom, what are you talking about?" she asked.

"I'm going to go get Lilly," Camille said with fervid determination.

Casey was in shock as she watched her mom grab her keys and her purse and start for the door.

"Mom...you can't. You can't go by yourself."

"Casey...I have to go get Lilly. She's in danger. I will not leave her there unprotected!"

"Okay, okay, Mom, I know...but I'm going with you," Casey said, equally determined.

"No!" Camille practically screamed, "Casey, don't argue with me, I won't have you both in danger."

Casey stood her ground, she was adamant, "Mom, you can't do this by yourself. I'm going with you!"

"She's right, Mrs. Castle," said Chance, already standing by the door, "you can't do this alone."

He quickly opened the door, "Let's go. I'll drive."

146

Cutahey's Lounge was again living up to its old reputation as a notorious breeding ground for "nothing but trouble." During its prime, some poor soul could easily wind-up paying a very high price just by dropping in for a tall, cool one or a fast hand of poker. Though the players frequently changed, the outcome rarely did. Any time trouble walked through its doors, someone inevitably ended up...busted-up, dying or dead.

This time, Mole found himself at the center of the fury and his chances of coming away unscathed were bleak. His circumstances had become increasingly threatened as J.C. continued to rage at him.

"You're nothing but a freakin' detriment," J.C. bellowed loudly. "I set you up. I lay out the plan. I put you in these accommodations. I do everything but hand carry the bags to you! And you still manage to screw it up!"

Frantically, Mole yelled out.

"J.C.! J.C.! It ain't as bad as it looks, man!"

Hoping to buy time, Mole scrambled for an explanation, "Look, look...I got a handle on where the stuff is, man. Give me a chance. I can make it right."

Hearing the admission, J.C. suddenly became very quiet and still. He walked over to Mole, closely scrutinizing him, "You sayin'...you got the stuff?"

Mole was sweating heavily, "Not here. But, I can get it."

"I'm listenin'," J.C. said calmly, "and this better not be another one of your scams. You get what I'm sayin'?"

The message was loud and clear to Mole. He quickly began his defense. "J.C., I swear to you, man, I'm not jerking with you."

Laughing nervously, Mole tried to ingratiate himself, "I'd have to be a total idiot to mess with you now, man."

J.C. was not convinced.

Sweating profusely, Mole anxiously went over to the bar. As he did so, Mandy's heart started to pound. Putting distance between herself and the bar, she cautiously eased over to Lilly and nervously held onto her hand.

She watched as Mole started anxiously searching for the key. Eagerly, he looked on the floor around the bar. Unable to find it, he looked up at J.C. J.C.'s face remained stone cold. Mole looked at Bull and Weasel.

"Where the hell's the key?!" he demanded angrily.

Blank faced, the two men shrugged.

Mole was starting to panic, "Which one of you idiots picked up the key?!

"Mole, we ain't seen no key," insisted Bull.

Knowing full well that he was in serious trouble, Mole looked at J.C again. Then, he looked at Mandy. It hit him like a bolt. His face turned beet red.

He practically hissed at her.

"Where is it?"

Mandy fearfully stepped behind Lilly's chair, "I...I don't know."

Infuriated, Mole started towards her, "Don't you lie to me you lousy, no good..."

He raised his hand, but was abruptly interrupted by the sound of cars skidding to a halt outside of the lounge. J.C.'s two bodyguards hurriedly drew their guns, eased over to the windows and cautiously looked through the cracks in the boards. They saw Colter and several deputies braced behind their cars with weapons drawn. One of the bodyguards glanced over his shoulder at J.C.

"It's the cops!" he alerted.

Mole opened a drawer behind the counter and took out three guns. He tossed one each to Bull and Weasel as the men took up positions.

Mandy hastily ducked behind the bar for safety. As Mole crouched next to a window, J.C. silently motioned to one of his bodyguards to check the back. The man did as he was told and headed towards the back of the lounge to secure the rear entrance. Bull and Weasel followed closely after him.

Jeff Colter's commanding voice could be heard over a bullhorn from outside.

"Do as we say and nobody will get hurt. Just send the girls out."

His demand was met with gunfire. The deputies returned the fire. Everyone in the lounge ducked for cover...except Lilly.

Colter yelled out to his men, "Hold your fire, we've got hostages in there."

Not one to miss an opportunity, Mole looked over at Lilly.

"That's right, we've got ourselves a little hostage." With one arm, he grabbed her out of her chair.

Glaring at him, J.C. gruffly ordered, "Put her down!"

"Like hell!" Mole said, incredulously. "This sweet, little girl's my ticket outta here." Ignoring J.C., Mole clutched Lilly tightly around the waist and moved towards the door.

Once at the door, he began to open it slowly.

Just as Mole moved Lilly into the open doorway into clear view, Camille, Casey and Chance drove up the driveway to the lounge. Mole tightened his grip on Lilly and pointed his gun at the deputies. Terrified, Camille jumped out of the car.

Colter yelled for her to stay back!

He quickly looked around at the deputies and cautioned them, "All right, everybody just take it easy."

Colter then called out to Mole, "Let her go."

It was the last thing Mole planned to do. He was ready to play his hand. Holding Lilly tightly up against him, he yelled out, "You got no say, Sheriff. You want this kid to keep breathin', you'll put your guns down and start walkin' back up that road towards the highway. You hear me!"

Mole placed his gun to the side of Lilly's head for emphasis. "Do it!"

Camille gasped as she and Casey watched in horror. Their horror turned to shock and confusion when they heard Colter issue his order to his men.

"Do as he says," Colter commanded, calling out to his deputies. "Everybody...guns down and move it," he ordered, "back up to the highway."

The deputies hesitated but then began placing their guns down and started walking away from the lounge as ordered. Astonished, Camille stood there in shock. She could not believe she was watching them all walking away and abandoning her young daughter. Just as she started to bolt forward towards the lounge to save Lilly, Colter grabbed her by the arm. Forcing her to come with him, he whispered in her ear.

"Camille, trust me. Keep walking. I've got men around back and the roads are blocked. He's not going anywhere."

Mole watched the lawmen start to disappear down the road, "That's right, boys, don't make 'ol Mole mad."

He loosened his grip on Lilly and looked down at her, "Well, little girl, looks like it's just you and me now," he smirked, "at least until Mole gets himself outta this mess."

Lilly looked around and sighed as if she were growing tired of the game. Seeing her reaction, Mole shook his head and laughed. "Man," he said, "you are one cool lil' cucumber."

"And, you're as dense as a brick," said a voice behind him.

Startled, Mole whirled around and pointed his gun as J.C. came out of the lounge.

"Oh, J.C., man," he said catching his breath, "I thought you had split." Lowering his gun, he looked at J.C., "Hell, man, you almost got yourself plugged. Ought not be sneakin' up like that."

"The kid's no threat to you. Let her go," he demanded.

Without emotion, J.C. drew his gun and pointed it at Mole.

Mole snickered, "What the hell you doin'? Huh? You gonna shoot me?"

"If I have to."

"Are you crazy, man," Mole tightened his grip on Lilly, "this ain't no time to be going soft. This kid's our only way out."

Practically growling, J.C. repeated the order, "I said... let her go."

Mole was not having any part of it, "Don't jerk with me, man!"

Both men suddenly flinched as gunfire erupted from the back of the lounge. They watched as one of J.C.'s bodyguards stumbled out from the side of the old bar and fell to the ground. More shots were fired. With J.C. distracted by the gun battle, Mole made his move. Gripping Lilly under one arm, he yanked her off her feet. Then, with a karate side-kick he knocked the gun out of J.C.'s hand, sending it flying.

Making a run for it, he bolted down the front steps towards the black Pontiac. When he reached the car, he shoved his gun into his belt, then opened the driver's door and threw Lilly into the front seat. Close behind, J.C. quickly caught up with him.

J.C. forcefully grabbed Mole by the shoulder and pulled him away from the car. The two men struggled violently. Pounding each other unmercifully with their fists, each became more and more bloodied as the fight continued. Soon, they were thrashing around in the dirt as each vied for the upper hand. Suddenly, in what appeared to be a death grip, they rolled one on top of the other, downhill behind the car. A shot was fired. Mole's gun had gone off. J.C. was hit.

Seriously wounded in the chest, J.C. continued to cling tightly to Mole. As Mole frantically struggled to shove him off, J.C. could feel the hot metal of the gun against his shoulder. Making a desperate grab for the gun, he was able to wrest it from Mole's hand. He continued to fight fiercely with his last remaining strength as Mole grappled to regain possession. As the two men rolled in the dirt, J.C. squeezed down hard on the trigger. The gun fired once, hitting Mole in the upper leg. J.C. then collapsed, seriously wounded.

Bleeding badly from his leg wound, Mole shoved J.C. out of his way and pressed his hand down hard on his leg, trying to stop the blood flow.

Grimacing, he managed to struggle up on his remaining good leg. With the blood still gushing out of his badly wounded thigh, he started back up the hill towards Lilly and the car. In a fury and gritting his teeth from the pain, he looked up and suddenly saw the last sight he would ever see -- *the black Pontiac was coming straight at him* with Lilly in the driver's seat. She had managed to slip the car in gear and was on her way, rolling backwards -- down the hill. There was a sudden, loud WHUMP as the car jostled, slightly.

Not having a clue what she had hit behind her, Lilly happily steered the car to a stop in some bushes at the foot of the hill.

When they heard the shots, Camille, Casey, and Chance, along with the deputies, raced in a dead-heat back towards the lounge. Camille saw Lilly in the car and rushed over to her. Casey was close behind when Camille opened the car door, grabbed her younger daughter and hugged her for dear life.

Chance stood protectively next to the three of them as the deputies fanned out to look for their suspects.

Colter and two of the deputies had surrounded Mole with their guns drawn. Colter reholstered his gun. It was clear the damage was done. Mole was no longer in any shape to harm anyone. He was dead.

Colter then went over to J.C. He could see the bullet wound in his chest. Colter stooped down to take his pulse. Having determined he was still breathing, he yelled out, "Somebody call an ambulance."

A deputy got on the radio to summon an ambulance as the remaining deputies surrounded the old lounge and scattered into the back woods in pursuit of the other thugs. Colter and two of the deputies, with guns in their hands, cautiously went inside Cutahey's.

Back in the protective care of her very much relieved family, Lilly smiled at her mom and her sister. She was very happy to see them. Camille and Casey looked at each other and then back at Lilly's sweet, little innocent face. Realizing how much danger she had been in, they broke into bittersweet tears of joy.

Camille reached over and caressed her daughter's face, "Angel, Mommie is so sorry. I should have never let this happen to you. Are you all right?"

Casey appeared disturbed by her mother's words.

"Mom, it wasn't your fault. It was mine. I was the one who was supposed to be watching her," she declared.

Camille looked at Casey. She could see how upset she was. "Sweetheart, it wasn't anybody's fault. There was no way we could know this was going to happen. Especially, to Lilly. The important thing, is that we were here for each other when it did."

Casey nodded her head, knowing her mother was right. Lilly looked at them both -- she didn't know nor care what all the fuss was about. As far as she was concerned, her day had been one big outing.

"Mom, do you think she knows what happened?" asked Casey as she looked over at Mole's dead body. Her stomach suddenly felt all queasy inside and she quickly looked away.

Camille shook her head, "No, sweetheart, I don't think so."

"Sometimes, I guess it's better not knowing," Casey concluded.

"Yeah. Especially when none of it was her fault," Chance added.

As Colter came out of Cutahey's, several deputies were bringing Bull, Weasel and the other bodyguard around to the front of the lounge in handcuffs. He watched his men load the prisoners into the squad cars when one of the deputies walked over and spoke to him in a low voice. Colter's expression changed slightly and he glanced over at Casey. He dismissed the deputy and started to walk in Casey's direction. He saw her looking around expectantly.

When Casey saw him coming towards her, she looked at Colter somewhat anxiously. "Where's Mandy?"

"She's gone," he answered.

"Gone?" Casey looked at him perplexed. "Gone where?" she asked.

"While my deputies were rounding up the prisoners, one of them saw her running off into the woods. I've sent a couple of men out to find her."

Casey was about to express her dismay when she was interrupted by the painful groans of the suspect lying on the ground nearby. Badly wounded and losing blood, J.C. was barely conscious. Struggling to hold on, he groaned again and called out.

"Camille..."

Astounded, they all looked at him. Camille gasped out loud. No one was more baffled than she at hearing this strange man call out her name. She stood there looking at Colter, unsure what she should do.

"Camille..." the man called out again.

This time, with Colter close by her side, she cautiously approached the wounded suspect. As she leaned down to get a better look at his face, Camille's knees practically buckled. She could barely believe her eyes.

"Joe?? Oh my God. Joe."

He looked up, straining to see her and asked anxiously, "Camille...?"

"Yes, Joe," she answered timidly.

"Lilly...is she all right?"

"Yes, Joe...she is. She's fine."

Relieved, the anxiety drained from his face. He turned his head to get a better look at Casey who was standing next to her little sister.

"Couple of swell lookin' kids."

"The best," said Camille.

Straining to get his words out, he continued, "Camille, when that girl in there said...that Casey was Lilly's big sister, I took one look and I knew right then that..." He groaned and coughed in pain. "There was..."

"Don't talk, Joe."

"There...there was no way, I was gonna let anybody hurt one of my girls."

Camille's eyes filled with tears. An old wound, deep inside, began to ache. It was as if she could feel the years of scar tissue being ripped away. She felt the familiar pain of a terrible loss -- the loss of a very young woman from a very long time ago. Joe Castle saw the hurt in her eyes. It was something not unfamiliar to him. He had seen the look a thousand times in his mind's eye.

"Camille..."

"Yes, Joe."

"I'm...I'm sorry."

Camille started to respond, but was interrupted by the sound of her daughter's voice. Casey stood there, looking down at her father. It was as if she were suddenly six years old again.

"Daddy," said Casey, barely able to speak above a whisper.

Her heart pounding, Casey kneeled next to her mother at her father's side.

"Daddy?" she said again, questioning, in disbelief.

Joe Castle struggled to see his daughter's face. It was stained with tears, just like the last time he saw her. His words came out with great difficulty as he fought for breath.

"Casey," he said, "you were right, sweetheart...I never should have left. It was a stupid..." he groaned in pain "...a stupid thing to do. I...I shoulda stayed."

He reached out for her hand. Frightened -- she, at first, hesitated.

How many times as a little girl had she imagined what it would be like to reach for her father's hand and feel the warmth and protection of his gentle grip? She looked down at him. She could see he was dying. Without further hesitation, she reached out. Little did she know, that in the end, it would be up to her to comfort him. Just as Casey took his hand in hers -- her father gasped his last breath.

Her hand begin to shake, uncontrollably. Without warning, long denied feelings welled up inside her. Her mind went numb as she looked down at the stranger before her.

She looked up at her mother and saw the look of despair on her face. No longer able to subdue her emotions, Camille let out a deep, painful sob. Struck by the sight of her mother's deep anguish, Casey instinctively wrapped her arms around her.

"Mom?!"

Camille looked at Casey. Tears were brimming in her eyes. She hugged her daughter tightly.

"It's all right, sweetheart," she assured her, "it'll be all right."

It was as if they both were reliving the past. Again, just the two of them, suffering the pain of loss. This time, as unexpected as it was, there was finally closure.

Camille took a moment to wipe her tears and then looked up at Colter. He reached out his hand. She took it, feeling the strength and security of his grasp. He gently helped her and Casey to their feet.

An ambulance pulled up and Camille and Casey went back to be with Lilly. Stunned by the odd turn of events, all they wanted to do at that moment, was hold on to each other tightly.

Colter stood over the body, looking down at Joe Castle, then over at the small family that he had given up -- and walked out on -- so many years ago. Through the thick and the thin of it, they were the strong ones, they were the ones who had survived.

A deputy walked over and stood beside Colter, interrupting his thoughts. The deputy cocked his head and looked down at the man lying dead in front of him.

"Who was that guy?" he asked.

Colter answered, matter-of-factly, "Somebody who made a big mistake."

"Yeah, I can see that," remarked the deputy.

Colter looked back at the little family that had once been a part of Joe Castle's life.

"You don't know the half of it," he said to the deputy.

14)   FRESH BREEZES

Like a gyroscope, life seems to have a way of finding its own center -- a way of getting back to normal. Not withstanding that normal -- being the relative term that it is -- always allows for considerable subjectivity. Regardless of how anybody cut it, for Casey and her family, things were starting to feel right again.

Several weeks had passed since that fateful day. And finally, on one bright, sunny Saturday morning, everything was as it should be at Casey's house. Lilly was plopped on the couch staring at cartoons on TV while her mom was in the kitchen washing the breakfast dishes. The house had a cozy feeling about it. It was one of those casual Saturday mornings when the only thing that needed to be done was to figure out how to spend the rest of the day.

As the television blared with the antics of "Rocky and Bullwinkle," Lilly sat watching the small screen. She was fixated on the cartoon's funny voices and raucous behavior as Rocky zoomed across the screen in his aviator cap and snappy looking scarf saving Bullwinkle from yet another perilous misadventure. Distracted, she looked up as Casey came in from outside carrying the mail. Casey walked over to the couch, took a moment to separate out the junk mail and handed it to Lilly.

"Here, Lilly," she said, "these are for you."

Lilly beamed as she took the various flyers from Casey and started looking through them. Lilly liked getting mail -- and since there was usually a spare flyer or two, she always got her fair share like everybody else.

Casey took the rest of the mail over to the table in the small dining area. She sat down and started to casually flip through it. Camille was still in the kitchen, busy pouring them each a glass of cold apple cider. She took a quick second to poke her head out and say, "If there are any bills, just stack them on my dresser, I'll deal with them tomorrow."

"Okay, Mom," Casey replied.

As Casey shuffled through the mail, she pulled out a small, white envelope and gasped.

Hearing her -- her mom asked, "Honey, what is it?"

"Mom, it's from Mandy."

Camille stopped what she was doing and went to her daughter's side. Casey quickly opened the envelope and pulled out a single piece of notebook paper. Casey eagerly read Mandy's letter out loud.

"'Dear Casey, Don't worry. Eddie came through for me.'"

Astounded, they both looked at each other, "Eddie?"

Casey continued to read, "'Thanks to him, I've got a few bucks to see me through...at least for a while. Let my folks know I'm okay and that I'll be in touch when I get some stuff worked out in my head. I promise....okay?

You're my best friend in the whole world and I want you to be the first to know. I'm doing the right thing. I'm having my baby. I love you, Case. Mandy.'"

"My, Lord, she's having a baby?!" exclaimed Camille.

Casey looked at her mom and nodded her head matter-of-factly.

"Yeah, Mom. She didn't want anybody to know."

Camille looked back at her daughter for a moment. The pieces of the puzzle began to fall into place in her mind. She looked at Casey and sighed.

"Well, thank God she's all right," she said without further comment on the subject.

"What's the postmark?" she asked.

Casey looked at her, "What?"

"See where it was mailed from."

"Oh," said Casey as she flipped the envelope over and looked.

"New Orleans."

"New Orleans? What in the world is she doing in New Orleans?" puzzled Camille.

158

"I don't know," Casey answered blankly.

"New Orleans is a sizable city," said her mom. "Far too easy for a body to get lost in, if you ask me." She then wondered out loud, "Wherever in the world would a boy like Eddie Burkette get enough money for her to live on?"

"I don't know," answered Casey. "I guess in his own screwed up way, Eddie came through for her after all."

"Frankly, I don't think 'Eddie' did her any favors. Seems to me, he helped make a mess of things."

"Mom?"

"What, sweetheart?"

"You think she's going to be all right?

"Oh, honey, it's hard to say," Camille sighed. "Considering she's pregnant, she's bound to come home eventually. Until then, we can only pray she's taking care of herself. But, right now, I think I'd better phone her parents and let them know."

"Mom?"

"What, sweetie?"

"You don't think that day at Cutahey's, Dad would have ever done anything to hurt her, would he?"

The question stopped Camille cold. She thought for a moment. Then answered her daughter honestly, "Casey, I don't have an answer for that. But, I can't imagine that he would. So, I think it'll be all right if we both decide that he wouldn't have."

Casey always liked her mom's openness. It had been a special bond between them for as long as she could remember. It seemed particularly important now that she was becoming an adult, even though there were times she still felt like a little girl. Especially when there were questions from the past that were still unresolved.

"Mom?"

"Yes, dear."

"Dad. He...he didn't forget us, did he?" asked Casey.

"No, sweetheart, he didn't."

"You think he ever thought about coming back?"

Camille went into the kitchen to get the cold apple cider. "I don't know."

159

She handed Casey her juice, took a glass over to Lilly and then sat down at the table. A melancholy look shadowed her face.

"Your dad chose a life that could only hurt us. He probably did the best thing for all of us by staying away."

Casey looked down at the table, "I just wish I could have known him. I never thought he even cared about us. I mean, if he did, he would have figured out some way to get in touch with us, right?"

"Maybe, maybe not. But, there is one thing I want you to always remember. You girls were the last thing on your father's mind before he died."

Her mom's comment eased Casey's pain. She shifted around in her chair.

"Mom, you ever wish it had worked out between you and him?"

"The way I see it," she said without hesitation, "your dad was there for me when I needed him the most. He saved Lilly."

Hearing her name mentioned, Lilly hopped off of the couch and brought her empty juice glass over to her mom. Camille took the glass and put it down on the table, then reached into one of the front pockets of her apron and took out a napkin. Casey watched as her mother pulled Lilly close to her and dabbed the excess cider off of Lilly's chin with the napkin. It was a scene she had seen dozens of times before with Lilly so innocent and trusting in her mother's protective arms. Until that moment, she realized it was one she had always taken for granted. But, no longer. Seeing them there safe, together, stirred warm emotions in Casey that seemed to flow to the very depth of her soul.

"You're right, Mom" she said, feeling the intensity of her love for them both, "I guess you could say he was there when we all needed him."

Camille stopped what she was doing and looked at Casey.

"You know, sweetheart, you are growing up to be a very wise young woman. I'm very proud of you, Casey."

Casey smiled, relishing the praise. "Hey, I learned from the best," she quipped.

Camille laughed at the high-handed compliment, "Well, thank you."

"Mom?" Casey said.

"Yes, dear?"

"I'm really proud of you, too."

It was one of those rare moments that delineates a person's life -- adding a simple yet priceless value that only love can provide.

"Honey, I realize that we've all been through some pretty tough times. But, I want you to know...it's never been hard being your mom. You girls mean everything to me. You always have."

Yes, indeed, it was a fine Saturday morning. Normal, it seemed -- at least in the Castle household was in and of itself a matter as simple as being loved.

With her chin cleaned and dried, Camille returned Lilly to the sofa to continue watching TV. As she did so, there was a knock at the front door. Camille looked at Casey, "Honey, will you get that? I need to call Mr. and Mrs. Banks."

"Sure," Casey replied as she hopped up from the table.

Her mother went to the phone and Casey went to open the front door. Her face lighted up as she let out a squeal, "Mrs. Eberworth!"

Casey was truly surprised. She stepped out onto the porch and gleefully hugged her dear neighbor. Mrs. Eberworth appeared radiant as she thoroughly enjoyed the reception. Chance stood next to his grandmother, smiling.

Casey looked at him, "Hi, Chance."

"Hi, Case," he responded.

As soon they entered the house, Mrs. Eberworth made a beeline for Lilly and gave her a big hug and a kiss. "Hello, my little Angel." Lilly was loving the attention. Mrs. Eberworth grabbed her by the hand and spun her around to get a good look at her.

"Well, sugar," she said, beaming, "you don't look too much worse for the wear. And, from what I hear, nobody can say that about the other fella."

Having completed her phone call and hearing Mrs. Eberworth's voice, Camille came into the living room and greeted her old friend with a hug, "Hi, Mrs. E. How you feeling?"

Mrs. Eberworth sat down on the sofa. Lilly plopped down beside her.

"Getting stronger everyday," she replied as she gave Lilly a hug. "Especially, now that I've come to the conclusion I got nothin' to hide."

Casey piped up, "Mrs. Eberworth, Mama never told me what was wrong with you. I asked her, but she never really said."

Mrs. Eberworth looked at her and said, "Honey, that was my fault. I had a lot to work out in my head and I didn't want to worry you none."

Casey looked at her expectantly.

Mrs. Eberworth continued, "Had a little round-about with cancer."

Casey was shocked.

"It's not something you exactly go broadcasting around town," Mrs. Eberworth explained. "I kept quiet about it 'cause some folks around these parts think they can catch my cancer just by breathing the same air." She shook her head. "Can't rightly blame 'em," she said matter-of-factly, "I suffered from the same notion till the doctors set me straight."

"Are you all right?" Casey asked anxiously.

"Honey, I'd like to tell you I'm fit as a fiddle," she said. "The truth is…it's a day-to-day thing." Then, with determination, "But, I'll tell you one thing, I'm not about to stay cooped up wearing big sweaters in the summertime like some women in my day. No siree-bob." Her tone turned serious, "Now, I admit, that durned operation took the starch right outta me. Yes, ma'am, it did. I got to feelin' down right sorry for myself. Took me a while, but I finally figured out I am none the less a female just 'cause I lost some of my feminine attributes."

She looked at them with the same old fire in her eyes, "Darn time everybody realizes -- that it don't change who you are and it sure as hell don't change what you are!"

162

Casey smiled broadly at Mrs. Eberworth's renewed spunkiness. Chance looked at her warmly. It was obvious that he was very proud of his grandmother. An attentive Lilly was just happy Mrs. Eberworth was there sitting beside her and scooted over to get closer to her. Mrs. Eberworth kissed Lilly on the forehead.

"Besides," she said looking at Lilly, "a lot of the world's got it much worse off than we do, don't they, Angel?"

Camille smiled, knowingly, "Amen."

Casey loved that about Mrs. Eberworth. She could find the good in the worst situations.

"Mrs. E," said Camille, "I know you've been through an awful lot with all of this. But, I just have to tell you how much I admire your attitude."

"Oh, honey, I have to admit, I didn't come to my conclusions on my own," Mrs. Eberworth confessed. "And, you're right, for a while I was having a pretty rough go of it until I learned a lesson from...the one-and-only...Mrs. Eleanor Hotch-kiss Creighton."

"Mrs. Creighton!?" Casey blurted out, surprised.

"That's right, Mrs. Creighton," explained Mrs. Eberworth. "You know, the Grande Dame of Cedar Grove society."

"Yes, ma'am," said Casey, "I know who she is."

"Well, not long ago," Mrs. Eberworth continued, "the poor woman had a pretty bad stroke. Paralyzed the left side of her face, rock solid. Can't budge it nary so much as an inch. But, the right side's okay and from what they say, so is the rest of her...both mind and body. Well, I hear tell she won't come out in the daylight. Stays cooped up in that big, 'ol house of hers, afraid people will point and stare at her unfortunate condition."

Mrs. Eberworth's story was far from being lost on Casey. Overwhelmed by the sheer irony of it, her mind raced back to the various painful encounters with Cedar Grove's "Grande Society Maven" that would have left a more fragile, young girl deeply scarred.

"That is just too weird," she said out loud, without thinking.

"Isn't it, though," continued Mrs. Eberworth to Casey. "But, I imagine she's doing her best to protect herself from some thoughtless fool's ridicule and pity."

Mrs. Eberworth looked directly at Casey, "After all, some folks can be mighty cruel for no reason at all. But, I say, the hell with insensitive folks like that. They ain't worth the time it takes to worry about them, are they?"

"No, ma'am," answered Casey soberly, "they're not."

Mrs. Eberworth looked at Casey warmly, "That's right, honey, they never have been and they never will be. Don't you forget it."

It felt good being with Mrs. Eberworth again. Talking with her always gave a person the feeling that somehow she knew far more than what she was letting on. But, then, reflected Casey -- it seemed she always did.

"I have an idea," exclaimed Camille, "if everybody's agreeable, why don't we all go to the restaurant for lunch today?"

"Why, Camille," said Mrs. Eberworth, "that is a splendid idea."

Casey and Chance exchanged glances. They found the suggestion to be highly agreeable.

"Great," said Casey.

"Yeah," said Chance, "sounds great to me."

It was perfectly fine with Lilly also. She beamed at Mrs. Eberworth as if she had rediscovered an old friend.

***

Downtown Cedar Grove was a buzz of activity on Saturdays. Cars lined the streets as people darted in and out of stores and various small shops making special purchases they had been unable to get to during the work week. It was the one day of the week when the local merchants could count on doing a volume business.

Anyone stopping in for a bite at Shey's Restaurant that fine day around noon time could have easily mistaken a group gathered in the back as one big, happy family. Though not altogether inaccurate -- it would, as yet, be a premature assumption.

Few folks could truly appreciate the events that had brought them all together. One thing was clear, however, it was their time to celebrate and anyone could easily see that it was a joyous occasion.

It was hard for Casey to remember a time when her mom had looked happier. As everyone sat around the big, round table near the back of the restaurant, they were genuinely enjoying one another's company.

To everyone's delight, the waitresses buzzed around the table serving the meal. As one of the waitresses handed Lilly a Coke, another one carefully placed a large bowl of hot chicken and dumplings in the center of the table.

Eyeing the sumptuous fare, Chance glanced at Casey and said, "I love chicken and dumplings."

"Me too," she said, her eyes lighting up.

Lilly downed her Coke and Casey watched as Mrs. Eberworth neatly tucked a napkin into Lilly's shirt collar. It was good seeing Mrs. Eberworth back in the swing of things. Realizing how much she had truly missed her, Casey seemed to value her time with her more than ever before.

She suspected the same could be said for Lilly. Feeling like her old self again, Mrs. Eberworth was as attentive to Lilly as a mama bird around a new born chick.

It was as if Mrs. Eberworth's operation had left her newly inspired. From that day on, she vigorously pursued what she called her campaign of enlightenment.

She said two things were needed to change people's minds when they were dead set on their own way of thinking -- a sensitive heart and the hide of a rhinoceros. And, it was evident to those who knew her well, that Mrs. Eberworth had long had both.

Mrs. Eberworth watched closely as Lilly relished the last sip of her Coke. Having turned the bottle upside down, completely draining it -- she chuckled to herself and said, "Lilly, honey, give it up. I'd say that bottle's as dry as the Sahara Desert."

Mrs. Eberworth motioned to a waitress to bring another one.

"Might be a good idea to keep 'em comin'," she advised.

The waitress smiled and went to get another Coke for a very thirsty Lilly.

Lilly never gave any indication that she had been adversely affected by her abduction and the subsequent ill fate of her kidnapper. Though the matter did eventually go before a court, she was never charged with vehicular manslaughter. The judge said something about "extenuating circumstances." But then, with Lilly, there always were.

Everyone looked up as Jeff Colter came into the restaurant. There was something about him, a new ease. One might suspect it was work related -- being that he had just locked up a bunch of bad guys. He had, after all, made Cedar Grove a safer place to raise a family. But, they would be wrong.

Colter walked over, kissed Camille on the cheek and then sat down and joined everyone at the table. Two waitresses who were closely eyeing the actions of Camille and the Sheriff, raised their eyebrows approvingly at one another as they continued to bustle around the table serving the food.

Chance and Casey blushed at one another as they too watched the exchange of affection. Flustered, Casey dropped her napkin onto the floor. Chance quickly reached down to pick it up. Then, as if it were second nature to him, he draped it casually across Casey's lap. When she reached down to secure it in place, her hand gently brushed against his. Feeling her touch, he let his hand linger next to hers for a moment and smiled.

Both Casey and her mother had managed to find two good men who wanted to be a part of their lives. Neither of them were sure how they got so lucky. All in all, it was a very special feeling. Though they both knew, that together, they had weathered some very tough times. And, somehow through it all, they had done just fine by themselves, thank you.

The funny thing about life is that everybody has to learn to deal with it on their own terms. As Mrs. Eberworth would always say, "Get over it and get on with it."

But then, that kind of home-grown, straight-out logic, didn't exactly apply to Lilly. Lilly's circumstances were all together different. Her terms were innocent, simple and trusting. Somehow her innocence was like a mirror, reflecting how messed up the rest of the world was. Like a little compass in life, she helped those around her figure out what was important and what was not. What a blessing she had been to her family.

As Lilly finished off her second Coke, each of the two waitresses quickly placed another one in front of her. Seeing the two Cokes sitting there, Lilly's eyes lighted up as she beamed up at the two waitresses.

Camille looked at her daughter, then said drolly to the waitresses, "I think you've just become her new best friends."

They all laughed the way family laughs when they know they are sharing a special time and a special space. In her wisdom, Mrs. Eberworth looked at them all, then smiled at Lilly, "The Good Lord had truly blessed you, my sweet, sweet child...with a dear and loving family."

She gently cupped Lilly's innocent and trusting face in her capable hands.

"But then," she continued, "who couldn't love such a little angel."

Casey could only imagine that there would be few times in her life that would be better than this. Funny thing, she thought to herself, how life could turn out...especially after it had seemingly dealt her such a bad hand.

At the time, her broken home and meager beginnings cast a shadow over the rest of her life. But, sitting there, she couldn't help smiling to herself as she watched the affection between her mother and little sister. The one thing that she would never underestimate was the love that bound her small family together. Through the thick and the thin of it, it alone had turned their impoverished past into a promising future.

For her, Mrs. Eberworth's words rang truer than ever.

"What a body has to remember, child...is to get over it and get on with it... whether it takes several years or just one day at a time."

And, that's what they did, both Casey and her mom. They turned Mrs. E's advice into a way of life. But, it was from Lilly that they learned the most valuable lesson of all. She taught them how to love and be loved unconditionally. And that...was nobody's burden. As time passed, it turned out that there was a lot to be learned about life in the small town of Cedar Grove. But then, a lot can happen on the backside of nowhere.

THE END

About the Author

Sharon Sebastian is a writer for Film, Television, Magazines and Books.

www.ingramcontent.com/pod-product-compliance
Lightning Source LLC
Chambersburg PA
CBHW031630110626
46523CB00055B/324